A READING OF E. M. FORSTER

A READING OF E. M. FORSTER

Glen Cavaliero

ROWMAN AND LITTLEFIELD
Totowa, New Jersey

© Glen Cavaliero 1979

First published 1979 by
THE MACMILLAN PRESS LTD
London and Basingstoke

First Published in the United States 1979
By Rowman and Littlefield, Totowa, N.J.

ISBN 0-8476-6191-1

Printed in Great Britain

for Bill

Contents

Acknowledgements

My thanks are due to the Provost and Scholars of King's College, Cambridge, for allowing me to consult the Forster archives in their keeping; to the Syndics of the Fitzwilliam Museum, Cambridge, for granting me access to Charles Sims's painting *The Little Faun*; and to Edward Arnold (Publishers) Ltd for their kind co-operation in the use of extracts from the works of E. M. Forster.

The wisdom of the heart having no concern with the erection or demolition of theories any more than with the defence of prejudices, has no random words at its command. The words it pronounces have the value of acts of integrity, tolerance and compassion.

Joseph Conrad, Nostromo

Introduction

The appearance of another book about E. M. Forster may seem to call for explanation, for since his death in 1970 nine volumes of the Collected Abinger Edition have been published, as well as three full-length critical studies and P. N. Furbank's invaluable biography. The sheer bulk of this material, however, testifies to the interest taken in Forster both as man and writer; and while he continues to draw readers – and he does – it may not be officious to add one more tribute to the pile.

The first one, supplied by Rose Macaulay in 1938, exemplifies the intimate approach which Forster's novels seem to invite. A personal friend, and a novelist herself, she shared his liberal background and, to some extent, his Cambridge associations. Her book constituted a salute and a dialogue, and where she disagreed with him she said so: the phrase 'Not true, of course' sounds through this otherwise appreciative study like a buzzer. The dialogue has been kept up by her more overtly academic successors, and their work establishes beyond a doubt just how complex and densely packed the relatively small body of Forster's writing is.

Indeed, his celebrated (and invented) epigraph to *Howards End*, 'Only connect', would seem to dog his critics, for he is an elusive novelist to 'place' or capture. His writings, while elaborate enough to warrant the exhaustive attention they have received, have a lightness of touch and tone that can make the commentator feel as clumsy and over-definitive as even Virginia Woolf had felt herself to be where Forster was concerned. She found him 'whimsical and vagulous to an extent that frightens me with my own clumsiness and definiteness'.[1] Twelve days later the impression is expanded:

He is fantastic & very sensitive; an attractive character to me, though from his very qualities it takes as long to know him as it used to take to put one's gallipot over a humming bird moth.

More truly, he resembles a vaguely rambling butterfly. . . .[2]

So how does one categorise him as one hovers, gallipot at the ready? As the liberal's spokesman or as a fantasist? As satirist or visionary, social commentator or poetic symbolist? As Edwardian or Modernist? Or as all these things? For with the publication of *Maurice* and the posthumous tales, and of the biography, other perspectives on the life and work have opened up. It begins to look as though in Forster's case, as in his own outlook, 'both/and' is to be preferred to 'either/or'.

Each of the above aspects of him appears, to a greater or lesser extent, in all the novels. Do they conflict? To follow one interpretation only is to suggest that they do (F. R. Leavis, for example, finding the moral seriousness compromised by the playfulness and fantasy);[3] but the very fact that so many different approaches have been persuasively argued would suggest either that they cancel out (in which case the whole process of critical examination is discredited) or that they are complementary. Forster himself, commenting on his own attitude to the Great War, throws light on the matter: 'Don't say "face facts" to me . . . it's impossible to face facts. They're like the walls of a room, all round you. If you face one wall, you must have your back to the other three.'[4] This sense of relativity prevented him from committing himself at any time to a dogmatic position. Only as an artist was he wholehearted, for it was only in art that he saw any real evidence that human beings have a capacity for harmony and order.

His ability to combine the various aspects of reality in one work of art is what makes him the writer he is, so teasing to the single-minded and dogmatic, and yet so rich in meaning and so perennially rereadable. Certainly the non-specialist reader, untroubled by critical dissension, has found this to be so: Forster is, I would guess, more continuously loved than any other major twentieth-century English novelist. Because they can be trusted, his books can be enjoyed in the same way as we enjoy the novels of Jane Austen.

As for this particular interpretation of his work, it does not pretend to be a piece of original research, nor is it a refutation of anybody else's book. It is offered for what it is – a reading, an interpretation of Forster's novels and tales in the context of his other work and against the background of what we know about his life and times. It also proposes a relationship between the nature of his message and the conditions under which it found expression.

Of necessity the biographical factor has to be taken into account. Forster is our one indisputably homosexual novelist of classic status, and the manner in which he made his own personal situation an occasion for more generalised social and philosophical statement is what justifies that status. In the wake of this contention I have interpreted the novels and tales as the imaginative ordering of certain conflicting personal insights and experiences; and as the stabilising of tensions and contradictions into a balanced and comprehensive mode of perception. Forster's novels exhibit a progressive consciousness of how we may best understand and bear the necessary pain involved in being human. Products, to a large extent, of personal frustration, they make of frustration a method of awareness that contains its own antidote. He is a novelist of containment: if he is a prophet he is one who speaks to our need for stillness rather than to our need for action. In this respect he is conservative in the fullest sense, standing as much at the end of the nineteenth-century tradition as at the beginning of the twentieth. Not for nothing did Lawrence say to him, 'To me you are the last Englishman. And I am the one after that.'[5] In that remark we can perceive the reason for the two men's mutual blend of admiration and mistrust.

I should like to record my warm thanks to Mrs E. E. Duncan-Jones, who read this book in manuscript and made many helpful comments and suggestions; to Mary W. McDougall; and also to the following, who have kindly assisted me in various ways: Mr Hugh Brogan, Mr P. N. Furbank, Mr Peter Gregory-Jones, Mrs Eileen Mable, Miss Elizabeth Poston and, by making me the present of a phrase, Mr Denis Yates. Mr Kenneth Hopkins has again generously been my proof-reader. Finally, I should like to acknowledge the help received from the various Adult Education classes with whom over a number of years I have discussed E. M. Forster's work in his own territories of Hertfordshire and Cambridge.

1 The Life

Forster's celebrated initials were the result of a mistake. Although at his birth he was registered under the name of his great-uncle, the banker Henry Thornton, at the christening his father in a fit of absent-mindedness supplied his own name, Edward, in its place. As things turned out the child was always to be called Morgan, so this hardly mattered; but the absurd little episode alerts us to an ambiguity. One part of him was Henry, the other Edward; one was conservative, serious, truthful and punctilious, the other was rebellious, humorous and unexpected.

To Henry we owe the profitable development of an impressive family background. The Thorntons belonged to that group of wealthy and high-minded friends who were once designated by Sydney Smith 'The Clapham Sect', and of whom the most celebrated member was William Wilberforce. The Wilberforces, Thorntons and Macaulays were evangelical in their Christianity, retentive, but not covetous, of their wealth, and inclined to be proprietorial in their relationships. By the time that Forster was born, on New Year's Day 1879, the family had dispersed from Battersea Rise, their spacious house on Clapham Common; and the only member left to have much influence on him was his great-aunt Marianne (Aunt Monie), whose biography was to be his last published book, and whose money enabled him to write the others without the distraction of having to earn a living. Forster owed a great deal to the Thorntons, not only in a material sense, and was always ready to acknowledge it.

His father, whose mother had been Aunt Monie's sister, died ten months after his son was born, and Morgan grew up in the sole care of his mother. Lily Forster (her real name was Alice Clara) was to be a dominant influence in her son's life, and he has been derided in some quarters for living at her apron strings; but the relationship between them was strongly companionable, and, it is impossible not to think, beneficial to his art. Her own

1

family, the Whichelos, were lively, a bit rackety, warm-hearted and hot-tempered, and the contrast between their world and that of the grave, responsible and piously materialistic Thorntons was to prove a fruitful theme in Forster's fiction, and one that he developed in surprising ways. If the solid nineteenth-century values of the Thornton family gave his works their underlying seriousness, the more contemporary Whichelos not only provided a moral counterweight, but also may have influenced the dexterous and elusive methods of his plots and narratives. Forster was the kind of writer who makes a myth out of his own life by weaving its various strands into a new pattern.

That pattern was the necessary product of his circumstances, and took the form, in the long run, of the resolution of a problem. The personal problem which he himself had in due course to face, the recognition and acceptance of his homosexuality, was to be the motivating force of much that he was to write; but this private crisis was symptomatic of far more. Forster had the intelligence and the imaginative energy to relate his personal life to the world from which it derived, and to enlarge the issues attendant on the one by demonstrating their relevance to the other.

His childhood and boyhood were dominated by women – his mother, his grandmother and her three other daughters, his great-aunt and her vinegary niece Henrietta Synnot; in addition there were his father's sister, Laura Forster, and even his mother's friend, Maimie Aylward, with her two sisters: it adds up to an alarming number. He was coddled and cosseted: his father's death made him the more precious, and he was encouraged to think of himself as frail. He had, he tells us, 'the deplorable nickname of The Important One'. We see him in one photograph, clad in Fauntleroy suit with lace collar and long curls; not surprisingly he was often taken for a little girl. His behaviour therefore inevitably showed a need to assert himself and a desire to please; and he developed a strong fantasy life, writing stories from an early age. Their titles are revealing: 'Chattering Hassocks', 'Scuffles in the Wardrobe', 'The Earring in the Keyhole'.[1] One sees prefigurations of the domestic disturbances in his early novels.

But the most significant element in his childhood was Rooksnest, the house in Hertfordshire which he was to make the model for Howards End, and to which he and his mother moved when he was four years old. It was just right – ancient but renewed, with modern comforts, and not too large. The garden contained the famous wych elm, and the property had its own patch of meadowland. In its small way Rooksnest constituted an estate. Lacking brothers and sisters, Morgan was thrown into the company of various garden boys, one of whom in particular was to remain important for his later emotional and imaginative life. Also there was the farm: if the yard with its stray animals alarmed him, the barn was a place which gave his imagination rein. This limited rusticity was enough to instil in him a love for rural England, though insufficient to make him a genuine countryman. Both his two home counties of Hertfordshire and Surrey were menaced by the sprawl of London, and in his early fiction he would make this semi-rural suburban world peculiarly his own. He is a novelist of borderlines and frontiers.

His attitude to urban growth was defensive. As he was to write in a later essay, 'I wonder what compensation there is in the world of the spirit for the destruction of . . . the life of tradition.'[2] The experience of change was for him a painful one: it is a feature of the early novels, of *Howards End* especially. Nothing in them appears to be static. All values, for good or evil, seem precarious.

When he reached the age for a formal education he moved into a different world. Eastbourne, on the Sussex coast, was notable then as now for the number of its preparatory schools. (George Orwell and Cyril Connolly were later to attend St Cyprian's.) Forster's school, Kent House, occupied buildings near the seafront, and it was there that he first experienced the pain of feeling himself an outsider. Prep-school boys are at the age when they are least imaginative and, as a result, most cruel. Inevitably the cherished Morgan suffered: he had not been encouraged to think of himself as hardy. Even so, he was eleven years old when he left home, older than the average new boy at a boarding school. His experiences were common enough, but he himself was not, and he reacted accordingly. A sense of incapacity before the world of affairs is a frequent legacy of such experiences, and there can be little doubt that Forster's ambiguous attitude to the practical Wilcoxes in *Howards End* stems in part from his early school experiences.

As to the sexual misadventure which befell him on the Downs, when he was 'interfered with' by a middle-aged man, it seems to

have ministered to his self-importance rather than to have produced any serious shock. He was more puzzled than frightened.
The spectacle he witnessed was probably less damaging than
the effect Forster's innocent disclosure produced upon his
mother. Having taught him to regard his own sexual organs as
potentially 'dirty', she was now almost as frightened as she
was embarrassed. The phrase 'What does it matter?', which
he was to employ tellingly in later years, could well have been
used by him at this time: it was in any case an expression much
in use by his favourite aunt, Rosie Whichelo. He had still more
occasion to cling to it when he went on to his public school at
Tonbridge.

This time he was a day boy; but all the same he was unhappy
there at first, bullied, and oppressed by the predominantly
athletic and conformist atmosphere. Later on, things improved,
but none the less his verdict on Tonbridge was to be negative.

> The best of life began when I left it, and I am always puzzled
> when other elderly men reminisce over their respective public
> schools so excitedly, and compare them as if they were works
> of art: it sounds as if they must have had a dullish time since.[3]

He has anatomised the system in *The Longest Journey*, concen-
trating on the snobbery and muddled thinking that, as he saw it,
lay behind the school's expansion from local grammar to public
boarding school.

> The change had taken place not so very far back. Till the
> nineteenth century the grammar-school was still composed of
> day scholars from the neighbourhood. Then two things hap-
> pened. Firstly, the school's property rose in value, and it
> became rich. Secondly, for no obvious reason, it suddenly
> emitted a quantity of bishops. The bishops, like the stars from
> a Roman candle, were of all colours, and flew in all directions,
> some high, some low, some to distant colonies, one into the
> Church of Rome. But many a father traced their course in the
> papers; many a mother wondered whether her son, if properly
> ignited, might not burn as bright; many a family moved to the
> place where living and education were so cheap, where day-
> boys were not looked down upon, and where the orthodox and
> the up-to-date were said to be combined.   (Ch. 4)

The wit is characteristic; so also is Forster's focus on the mystique of the school system. He will not expose the practice of bullying unless he can get at the cause of it. Unhappy he may have been, but his account of his old school is devoid of self-pity.[4]

After he had left school, his mother moved to Tunbridge Wells, five miles away, from which (with Weybridge, their later home) aspects of his fictional 'Sawston' are presumably drawn. (The name itself was taken from that of a village outside Cambridge, a disobliging act on the author's part.) During his Cambridge years Tunbridge Wells was his official home, and he disliked it greatly: the dullness, small-mindedness and snobbery of a society consisting largely of old ladies was in painful contrast with the liberal and masculine companionship which he enjoyed at Cambridge.

He went up to King's in 1897. The next three years were to be momentous for him, and in the course of them he found himself as a personality. This was a gradual process; he was never one for self-advertisement, but he was in a congenial atmosphere, which encouraged the flowering of unobtrusive people – provided that they had genuine intelligence and character. He read Classics first, then History, and achieved Second-Class Honours in both. But his studies were not the dominant element in his life at King's, though it was soon clear that he had an independent mind. He does not seem to have been over-impressed, for example, by the celebrated Oscar Browning. Far more influential were his Classics tutor, the formidable, atheistical Nathaniel Wedd, and the quieter figure of Goldsworthy Lowes Dickinson, whose biography he would later write. Dickinson was the quintessence of a certain kind of Cambridge don, and certainly constituted a Forsterian ideal. Shy, scholarly, discreetly homosexual, warm-hearted but with a razor-sharp mind, he embodied qualities which in due course came to be associated with Forster himself. Under his influence the latter gradually shed those Christian beliefs which he had in any case only vaguely held till then. He never recovered them, nor (more to the point) did he ever show any wish to do so. Their loss was, for him, the first stage in his inward liberation.

In 1901, during his fourth year at King's, he was elected to the Apostles, as the Cambridge Conversazione Society of 1820 had long been known: this marked his acceptance into the highest circle of Cambridge intellectual life. He took his place in a succession which had included not only such early nineteenth-century celebrities as Tennyson, Arthur Hallam, Monckton Milnes and F. D. Maurice but also the by-now influential figures of G. E. Moore, A. N. Whitehead, Henry Sidgwick and Roger Fry. The feeling of his own independence and achievement must have been strong in him: certainly his creativity was encouraged, for it was at this time that he began tentatively to experiment with the writing of a novel. Three drafts survive, and show that the preoccupations evident in *The Longest Journey* and *A Room with a View* were there from the start. At the same time he was in love with his sponsor to the Apostles, Hugh Meredith, and his love was, to some degree, returned. Certainly he was now able fully to acknowledge his own sexual nature: his problem subsequently would arise not so much from guilt as from shyness. He shed his religious beliefs more easily than his natural modesty.

But at Cambridge Forster discovered his ideal civilisation. One side of his nature was entirely satisfied; and the courts of reason, calm fair-mindedness, and warmth of heart were to be his refuge in later years and his inspiration at all times. A lesser man would have rested at that, and in that. But Forster needed more: as his novels came out their fierceness and oblique passion dismayed his relatives, though they were less surprising to his friends.

The years that followed his departure from Cambridge were unsettled. In 1902 he undertook a weekly class in Latin at the Working Men's College, where he continued to teach for over twenty years. But apart from this he did not have any regular employment, and was thrown back on house-hunting with his mother, and on beginning a new novel, the earlier attempts having come to nothing. In 1905 his frustration and sense of indirection led him to accept the post of tutor to the children of the Gräfin von Arnim, who lived in a large country house in Pomerania. The Gräfin, an Englishwoman, was a cousin of Katherine Mansfield and herself a writer, being the author of the anonymous and extremely popular *Elizabeth and Her German Garden* (1898). By the time Forster joined the household she had three more books behind her and was working on a fifth. A capricious, high-spirited woman with a streak of cruelty, she provided Forster with a female opponent who tested his self-confidence, and whose friendship he was, a little to his own dismay, to win. But he did not allow the friendship to become reciprocal. Correctly diagnosing her overriding need to be liked – a need which damages her potentially sharp-sighted novels – he found her untrustworthy and emotionally dishonest, and as a result withheld approval. He felt no corresponding urge to be liked himself.[5]

The tutorship behind him, he returned home to achieve a measure of literary fame. His novel *Where Angels Fear to Tread* came out in 1905, and was favourably received; and *The Longest Journey* (1907) and *A Room with a View* (1908), without selling particularly well, maintained his reputation. But his real triumph was *Howards End*, which appeared in 1910. The reviews were almost entirely enthusiastic, and he found himself regarded ' as 'among the writers whose work counts for something'.[6] It was even proposed to nominate him to the Royal Society of Literature. But, literary lionising holding no pleasures for him, he did not encourage it in others; nor were his own high standards satisfied. His moment of complete success ushered in a period of literary frustration.

The years between his own time in the German Garden and the Schlegel sisters' occupation of the garden of Howards End had been taken up with writing not only novels, but also short stories, essays and reviews. He travelled, frequently with his mother, in France and Italy; earlier, without her, he had been to Greece. But the only lasting effect of that visit, he complained, was a permanently red nose. His love affair (if one can call it that) with Hugh Meredith faded with the latter's marriage, though it was to have a brief revival in 1910. Far more important to him now, however, was the growing friendship with a young Indian, Syed Ross Masood, who came for a while in 1906 to be tutored by Forster at the house in Weybridge. Masood was everything that Forster was not: large, handsome, boisterous, volatile, enormously active, extrovert. Forster was soon in love, but, when he nerved himself up to declare his affection, Masood seemed scarcely to comprehend.

The frustration this caused was frequently apparent: his journals of the time show some painful entries.

Can I do anything? To screw up the will power by discipline is not possible, but could I become spiritually more solid? It's an extra difficulty with mother too, now that I know she does not think highly of me. Whatever I do she is thinking, 'Oh, that's weak.'[7]

His first visit to India was really precipitated by such questioning. It was to prove marvellously fruitful.

What Forster found in India was a species of deliverance that, precisely because its quality was so unexpected, was the more complete. He had always been a natural traveller, with a detached but responsive attitude to architecture and scenery (his guidebook to Alexandria, published in 1922, is a classic of its kind). In India, however, he found a landscape that defeated all expectation – a sense of space, an upending of priorities, an inconclusiveness that simply disregarded all the sharp divisions and antitheses that had made up his intellectual and emotional life. (The sharp differences within Indian life itself, not affecting him directly, were subsumed by him into the general atmosphere.) This enormous relativity constituted an alarming challenge to him, as the Marabar chapters of *A Passage to India* were to make clear; though that book in its totality would show that he could meet it. Surprisingly, his time with Masood would seem in the long run to have been less important than that spent with the Maharajahs of Dewas Senior and Chhatapur. The former was to invite him back to India in 1921; the latter, with his intellectual curiosity and freedom from European scruple, was to give Forster that vision of sublime confusion in Indian life which was to provide the resolution for his finest novel.

But another novel was to be written first. The Indian experience evidently led him to feel the need for a franker reckoning with his own sexual nature. Accordingly, while his mother was taking the cure at Harrogate (the collocation seems peculiarly appropriate), Forster took the opportunity to visit Edward Carpenter, pioneer prophet of sexual emancipation and apostle of the virtues of homosexual love, who was living at Milthorpe, near Sheffield. The result of this meeting was the writing of *Maurice*, unpublishable at the time, but a means of mental clarification for its author. One says 'mental' advisedly, for, as later critics were to point out, the sexual element in the book is muted. Forster may have hoped that it would free him to write another novel in the manner of *Howards End*, but the novel he attempted, 'Arctic Summer', hung fire: *Maurice* had provided merely an intellectual liberation. But at this time, in order to satisfy himself, he also began to write erotic tales with homosexual themes; and these may in the long run have proved more beneficial to his imagination, the ones which have survived showing a good deal more feeling for physical realities than does the high-minded and serious novel.

It was in this state of costive literary performance that the Great War was to uproot him. Unlike the generation of Rupert Brooke and Julian Grenfell (both of them young men with dominating mothers), he did not welcome it as a resolution of spiritual frustrations. These, he knew, lay within himself. Forty years later, writing of *Howards End*, he was to diagnose what had been wrong.

> Have only just discovered why I don't care for it: not a single character in it for whom I care. . . . Perhaps the house in *H. E.*, for which I did once care, took the place of people and now that I no longer care for it, their barrenness has become evident. I feel pride in the achievement, but cannot love it, and occasionally the swish of the skirts and the non-sexual embraces irritate. . . .[8]

They have irritated certain readers ever since the book appeared.

Like many of his fellow intellectuals, Forster was sickened and appalled by the outbreak of the war, viewing it along with D. H. Lawrence and the Bloomsbury writers as being the first plunge down the slopes of Gadara: his optimistic political liberalism never recovered from it, and his distrust of humanity in the mass grew stronger. His initial work, that of cataloguing books in the British Museum, though it was not a protest, might have been interpreted as one; for himself, 'doing' as distinct from simply 'being' must have seemed a necessity. More genuine action was to come: he served with the Red Cross in Alexandria between 1915 and 1919. Here, temporarily emancipated from home and mother, he was reasonably happy, making friends with C. P. Cavafy, whose poems he was to champion, and writing both the essays that were to be published in *Pharos and Pharillon* (1923) and also the excellent guidebook to the city, which, as for Lawrence Durrell after him, was to be a source of romantic fascination. It was also to be the scene of his first consummated love affair. This was with Mohammed el Adl, a young bus conductor, some of whose characteristics were to be incorporated in the person of Aziz in *A Passage to India.*

On Forster's return to England he became for a brief while literary editor of the *Daily Herald*, the war having made him increasingly sympathetic to the cause of socialism. He had many friends among the Left, Leonard Woolf and Sidney and Beatrice Webb being the most celebrated. His essay on the last two is notably just and balanced: indeed, Forster's political writing and activity was by no means the least of his work. But journalism, of however serious and committed a kind, was not a satisfying outlet for a writer whose creative impulse was still unfulfilled.

At last the catalyst arrived; in 1921 he returned to India to act as temporary secretary to the Maharajah of Dewas Senior. Much of what took place then is set down in *The Hill of Devi* (1953). Previous attempts to record his Indian experiences in the form of a novel had been unsuccessful; but now, his own pessimism and sense of inner social disaffiliation having been confirmed by the public events of the past ten years, he was able to generate enough imaginative energy from this and from his own sexual release to produce what is by common consent his masterpiece. For *A Passage to India* (1924) really does deserve the word 'definitive', at any rate where Forster's art is concerned. After it there was nowhere, in terms of fiction, for him to go. Middle age (he was now forty-five) and disenchantment with Western society and politics did the rest. It is small wonder that he wrote no more novels.

The life that he did lead was modest, but more useful than some people, conscious of his private income, might allow. His career in the 1920s was mainly literary. He gave the Clark Lectures at Cambridge in 1927, and published them under the title *Aspects of the Novel*. Audiences were enthusiastic – though the applause was not unanimous. F. R. Leavis found the lectures 'intellectually null';[9] and indeed their rather playful amiabilities were out of tune with the rigorous requirements of the critics who came after him. Forster's literary reputation has ever since been rather an uncertain quantity, though the debate has proceeded less along the lines of 'Does one rank him high or low?' as of just how high he really deserves to stand. And certainly such strictures as there have been have had little effect on his readers, who have been drawn from all ranks and age groups.

In the 1930s, along with many other writers (W. H. Auden,

Stephen Spender and George Orwell come immediately to mind), Forster found his literary concerns overshadowed with political anxieties, and he began to lay the foundations of that reputation as a humanist sage which was to revive interest (if a shade misleadingly) in his early writings. As Laurence Brander writes in his sympathetic study, 'in a decade of Leaders, he led our young writers, a humanist in a world of idealist communists and High Churchmen'.[10] To Auden and his circle Forster had become a kind of spiritual mentor, Christopher Isherwood writing in warmly affectionate terms of what he stood for at the time of the Munich crisis:

> *my* England is E. M.; the anti-heroic hero, with his straggly straw moustache, his light gay blue baby-eyes and his elderly stoop. Instead of a folded umbrella or a brown uniform, his emblems are his tweed cap (which is too small for him) and the odd-shaped brown paper parcels in which he carries his belongings from country to town and back again. While the others tell their followers to be ready to die, he advises us to live as if we were immortal. . . . He and his books and what they stand for are all that is truly worth saving from Hitler; and the vast majority of people on this island aren't even aware that he exists.[11]

Later still, after Forster's death, Isherwood was to write that 'A Forster novel taught Christopher the mental attitude with which he must pick up the pen.'[12] The anti-heroic hero was, indeed, to be a powerful influence on later novelists.

In 1932 Forster paid a visit to Rumania[13] (Italy he refused to visit while Mussolini was in power). 1934 saw not only the publication of his biographical tribute to Lowes Dickinson, but also his election to the presidency of the Council for Civil Liberties, a position which he held for three years. In the thirty years following the publication of *A Passage to India* he wrote no less than '348 articles, reviews and letters to the press; forewords or introductions to 43 books and a filmscript . . . was interviewed at least six times, and lent his signature to 16 open letters to the press'.[14] He came to the defence of Radclyffe Hall's novel about lesbianism, *The Well of Loneliness*, when it was prosecuted on its publication in 1929 – despite his probable disapproval of its emotional, unhappy ending, in such marked contrast with the one he had devised for *Maurice.* He also, and more dramatically, appeared in the witness box at the *Lady Chatterley's Lover* trial twenty-one years later. He was at all times an opponent of literary censorship. He served as President of the Humanist Society, and was a frequent lecturer on university platforms and at literary conferences. His address at the International Congress of Writers at Paris in 1935 is well known, having been reprinted under its title 'Liberty in England' in *Abinger Harvest* (1936), and is notably at odds with the increasing dogmatism and belligerency of the times. In addition to all this he was much in demand as a broadcaster, and found in wireless talks a medium for which he had prepared through the years of teaching at the Working Men's College. It suited him as perfectly as it was to suit the very different styles of Max Beerbohm and J. B. Priestley.

Through all this time he continued to live with his mother, at Weybridge and, following the death of his aunt Laura Forster in 1924, at Abinger Hammer in Surrey, a village now permenently associated with his name, and the subject of his most eloquent and deeply felt elegy upon the English countryside.[15] He did, however, escape from this close domestic tutelage to the extent of having a flat in London, where he could enjoy the companionship of a group of homosexual friends that included J. R. Ackerley and William Plomer. In this society he was able to break through the class barriers which oppressed him in his life at home; and in it too he was to find belatedly a measure of sexual and emotional happiness. It certainly bore little relation to the bookish world of publishers and parties inhabited by the majority of famous authors, and which was so deplored by Virginia Woolf (even while she was mixing in it herself). This detachment was something that she admired; and William Plomer has commented with likeable modesty that 'I believe not one of his closest intimates has ever been eminent in a worldly sense.'[16]

After the death of his mother in 1945 at the age of ninety, and his subsequent (and sharply contested) ejection by the landlord from his home at Abinger, Forster accepted an Honorary Fellowship at King's, and lived the rest of his life in Cambridge, a revered and popular celebrity. His old age was as tranquil and happy as old age can in its nature be. His intellectual powers did not diminish. *Marianne Thornton* (1956) and his last story, 'The Other Boat', completed in 1958 when he was just on eighty, are among the best things he ever wrote; while between 1949 and 1951 he had collaborated with Eric Crozier on the libretto of Benjamin Britten's opera *Billy Budd*. (He had taken an active interest in the Aldeburgh Festival from its inception, lecturing at the first one on George Crabbe, and on a later occasion giving a reading from his unpublished fragment 'Arctic Summer'.) In 1953 he was made a Companion of Honour (he had already declined a knighthood) and his ninetieth birthday coincided with the award to him of the Order of Merit. No less than sixteen critical studies of his work were published in his lifetime, as well as numerous essays, critical articles and appreciations; while the posthumous appearance of *Maurice* and the stories in *The Life to Come* (1972) have ensured that interest in his writing has been extended beyond its purely literary aspect. His last illness was free from pain, and he died on 7 June 1970 at the home of the married couple who had been his closest friends for many years. The relationship had begun on Forster's part as a romantic passion for the husband; it grew to include a no less deep attachment to the wife. The resolution of so potentially disastrous and painful a situation was itself a proof of the validity of Forster's personal ideals and aspirations, and witnesses to the possibility of their being put into effect. In this final friendship the man and the artist were at one.

2   The Background

Forster's novels and tales are full of memorable places. Atmosphere is what interests him most: the spiritual qualities of India, Wiltshire, San Gimignano are conveyed to us more vividly even than the physical. So in his own life we are made aware of Cambridge and Surrey as moral and intellectual climates, and the impact of the physical appears to have been overpoweringly strong only where his childhood home was concerned – Rooksnest, known to us as Howards End.

An old timber-built, brick-faced farmhouse on a hillside to the north-east of Stevenage, it is lovingly described by him in *Marianne Thornton.* No other place meant so much to him, and in his later years, following the move to King's, he was to use it as a retreat from which even intimate friends would be excluded. The house is the epitome of homeliness, unremarkable without, save for a bricked-in window where no window needs to be (no room for no view), but gracious and comfortably enclosing as you step inside. The wide view to the west towards the flat lands of Bedfordshire gives a sense of airy exposure, modified by the trees that protect the house to the north. Broad open fields suggestive of strip cultivation and the former commons, a hint of parkland, the church spire of Old Stevenage, the neighbouring farm – all these add up to an apparently timeless pastoral scene. But the scene now borders on the housing estates and factories of Stevenage New Town, and a vast hospital, at once menacing and reassuring, rises like Philip Larkin's 'The Building'[1] from the plain below. These new developments were not foreshadowed when Forster was a boy; but his sense of rural England was alive to their possibility. Compared with the Surrey woodlands of Abinger, settled and protected by the villas of Edwardian businessmen, this landscape is open, utilitarian in the true sense, and austere. It is Hertfordshire rather than the Home Counties south of London that was to be Forster's abiding spiritual ambience, the country to which he was constantly to return in

14

mind and body.

But, if Rooksnest enshrines the positive elements in Forster's personal myth, Eastbourne, where he went to his preparatory school, may serve as an architectural illustration of the world in which he grew up, and against which he was to react, both in love and anger, as his imagination deepened. Indeed, in recent years the place has become still more relevant to his concerns; for, just as he found himself caught between the claims of feudalism and socialism when, on being ejected from Abinger by the local squire, he found Rooksnest menaced by the urban fruits of left-wing policies, so the fine proportions of Eastbourne sea-front have been wrecked on the one hand by a tower block of luxury flats growing into the clouds (often quite literally) through the enterprise of private capital, and on the other by the steel and glass holiday centre of the Transport and General Workers' Union, rammed down among Victorian hotels like a huge mailed fist.

But despite these architectural solecisms the town still gives one a feeling of the world in which the young Forster grew up, an image in brick and stone of a particular phase of English history. Looking down from Beachy Head one is aware of the class divisions attested by the tree-lined residential roads of the wealthy and the grid plan of the terraced houses in the working-class quarter down by Langney marsh. Tiled roofs, copper cupolas and flagpoles obtrude through the trees, while ranked along the sea-front are the imposing bulks of the hotels, their very names evocative of imperial prosperity and power – the Cavendish, the Albemarle, the Burlington, the Grand. Behind them are five-decker houses of the late Victorian epoch, merging into the red-and-white doll's house type of the Edwardian age and later. Here the worlds of Sawston and Anglo-India seem to meet.

Eastbourne was, and from an architectural standpoint still is, an embodiment of what G. K. Chesterton once called 'The Victorian Compromise'[2] – that endeavour to reconcile the traditional social and religious order and beliefs with the methods followed to secure the nation's new economic prosperity. For instance the railway station (of confused Persian and Germano-Gothic design), testified to the far-flung nature of English power and prestige; the Town Hall (Free Renaissance) confidently proclaimed a prosperous future. The churches varied between G.

E. Street's lofty red-brick Anglo-Catholic St Saviour's (where Mr Borenius in *Maurice* might have been a 'Father') and the spindly early Gothic of Decimus Burton's Holy Trinity (Low Church, as was St Peter's, Tunbridge Wells, attended by Miss Charlotte Bartlett), while All Souls, Italianate in appearance but evangelical by persuasion, was an enactment in brick and stone of the soul of Philip Herriton. But the most momentous building went up ten years after Forster left the town – the Free Library and Technical Institute, the wide façade of which, flanked by towers and approached by a palatial flight of steps, confronted the wealthier visitors with the extension of their cultural inheritance to the class whose work supported it.

This building was the product of policies inaugurated by the Education Act of 1870, passed, nine years before Forster was born, by Gladstone's Liberal administration, which had laid the foundation of the society which all left-wing sympathisers of the moderate 'liberal' kind regard as just and democratic.[3] Indeed, in the mid nineteenth century the term 'liberal' was largely synonomous with that of 'Liberal' in a political sense; but by the time Forster came to maturity the two words had parted company. Division in the party itself, notably over the Home Rule question and the Boer War, led to the separation of private, personal liberalism from the field of political action. But liberality of outlook had had its origins in protest not only against the injustice and squalor of industrial England, but also against the moral and aesthetic philistinism of its perpetrators. Thus, while Matthew Arnold and John Ruskin had been eloquent on the contemporary indifference to beauty and decency in the growth of the industrial landscape, they had also voiced a concern over the moral complacency of the middle classes which was to be echoed in different ways by Shaw, Butler, H. G. Wells – and in due course by Forster himself. The idea died hard that the social order would improve as a result of growing enlightenment among the bourgeoisie and better living conditions for the poor: it was indeed part of the legacy of the Utilitarian philosophy that underlay the Industrial Revolution. We can see these questions exercising the minds of Forster's Schlegel sisters in *Howards End*. More and more people were living off unearned income: money from invisible sources accumulated, taking on a life of its own since the prevailing ethic dictated that it was more virtuous to save than to spend. Forster, himself a man of private means, was awake to the anomalies of the situation and was prepared to outrage contemporary taboos (money was no more to be talked about than sex) by discussing openly the relationship between morality and its financial props.

Among the enemies of moral and intellectual progress was that dogmatic puritan spirit castigated by Arnold under the nicely apt umbrella term of 'Hebraism'. The bulk of the Established Church, in the first half of the reign at any rate, was still evangelical in temper; but both the earnest humanitarianism exemplified by Henry Thornton the elder, and the spiritual ardours of early Methodism (which the Thornton temperament distrusted) had by the end of the century largely faded out, owing to the coincident impact of the businesss mentality among an increasing number of church-goers, and, among the lesser clergy, of the Tractarian movement. Certainly as the century progressed the imaginative energy of Christianity suffered as much as it gained from being forced into a departmental role. The forward-looking writers were all agnostics in one form or another, and a feeling for the supernatural was fed into the lives of the majority of them, Forster included, from sources other than orthodox Christianity. Forster's early novels arise out of a world where the springs of conduct are being radically questioned and people are looking for religious surrogates to sanction traditional moral standards, both through specific beliefs and through imaginative explorations. But old values were crumbling before new ones could be established. So long as education was the prerogative of the well-to-do, society might hope to be relatively stable, but the lower-paid were now as impatient of the social injunctions which a ruling caste had laid down for its own benefit as they were of its intellectual and ethical standards.

These standards, however, were not always anachronistic or unimaginative; and in many respects they were the standards that Forster was brought up to hold or which he acquired for himself at Cambridge. The study of the Classics, the cult of the individual spirit implicit in the reading of philosophy and the observance of religion, were furthered by the educational system inaugurated by Thomas Arnold earlier in the century and later attacked by Forster himself, by Lytton Strachey and by other of his friends in Bloomsbury. Thanks largely to the public schools (as Forster was to show) these standards, along with much else far less creditable, in part survived two world wars; but they remain what they were already beginning to appear in the 1890s, the property of a caste, albeit one with powers of apparently perpetual self-renewal. In the 1880s and 1890s the young were being taught to prize 'the things of the spirit' above worldly prosperity; but when they went out into the world they realised that the former were unobtainable without the latter. If you desired what the Hebraistic mind considered to be spiritual, that is to say gentility and scholarship, you must have cash: the fates of Hardy's Jude Fawley and Forster's Leonard Bast were common ones. In order to make the best of himself by these standards of cultural excellence, the average youth needed more money than he could lay his hands on, and was tempted to sacrifice to the means of getting it the very qualities which would make the rewards of his work worthwhile. The dilemma was to concern Forster acutely in the most panoramic of his early novels, *Howards End*.

As for the glittering sophisticated Society world of Edwardian London, it reflected not only a decline in the economic state of the old county families, but also an influx of transatlantic manners and international business interests. And yet the world of 'Society', which monopolises so much fiction of the period, seems cut off and isolated from what were in the long run the more momentous changes that were happening in the middle-class society which Forster chose to portray. And in the country, traditional repository of 'the timeless', change was greater still. Class distinctions, an obsession at all times with middle-class people, had had a certain meaning when country life had rooted them in a common tradition and given them a common aim – of sorts; but, with suburban development and the growth of the commuter way of life, this close-knit interdependence of classes was broken up. The process is described poignantly by 'George Bourne' (Sturt) in *Change in the Village* (1912) and elsewhere, and by Flora Thompson in the justly popular *Lark Rise* (1939). Here we may read of the people among whom Mrs Wilcox grew up at Howards End. Forster was to be sensitive to what was happening in the country; but he had no close acquaintance with rural life. His novels, though responsive to scenery, are not much concerned with agriculture: the one farmer to appear in them, the father of Stephen Wonham in *The Longest Journey*, is a romantic figure existing half way between the world of George Meredith and that of Mary Webb.

But coupled with the decline of agricultural life there was a corresponding change of a more elusive kind which touched Forster more nearly. The Wordsworthian vision of nature as being reciprocally in harmony with man was assaulted by the findings of mid-nineteenth-century science. The awareness of life as a continual struggle, coupled with the impact of Darwinism, seriously called in question the old liberal ideals. The effect of Darwinism upon orthodox religion is probably less important than its demonstration of man's animal origins, with all that that implied for moral idealism. While the new perspective on the universe produced gloom and fatalism in writers such as Thomas Hardy, who viewed human life as a maladjusted accident, others saw in the struggle for existence an endorsement of humanistic ideals. This was a view which Forster was in his more optimistic moments to endorse, though in other moods he appears more sympathetic to the pessimism of Hardy. But the new scientific perspectives did call for some kind of philosophical response: especially were they calling in question traditional notions about self-fulfilment. For the older, pre-scientific culture had been a laborious personal acquisition; human life had been interpreted as the response of the individual soul to its Maker, the Protestant doctrine of Grace with its emphasis on subjective apprehension encouraging a stringency of life and a direction of energies towards the realisation of God's Kingdom upon earth. Here indeed we find the religious origins of that idealistic liberalism with which Forster was to be identified.

But by the end of the century the growth of scientific knowledge, coupled with the new methods of industrial production, the beginnings of mass education and the development of communications meant that the concept of society-as-a-whole took on a greater and more generally applicable significance. The religion of the state seemed likely to replace the religion of the soul as the moral point of reference; the life struggle was seen as material rather than as spiritual, and collective rather than individual. This materialistic outlook was something which the young Forster questioned; but he was to question it on his own terms. As he was to write in 1946, 'The education I received in those far-off and fantastic days made me soft, and I am very glad it did, for I have seen plenty of hardness since, and I know it does not even pay.'[4] Though in the tradition of Arnold and Ruskin, he speaks with his own voice, not with theirs.

This evolutionary revolution (if the term may be permitted) was also responsible for the challenging of the traditional Victorian reticence concerning sex, a reticence that contrived to combine sentimental idealism where women were concerned with the implanting of guilt in the physical desires of men. Divorce, not warfare, between flesh and spirit resulted in the treatment of the primary human instinct as distressing, unmentionable and retrogressive. The reaction against this attitude in writers such as Swinburne and Oscar Wilde, who made tentative (and in the latter's case disastrous) investigations into the fields of sensation, did not amount to a correction of it; indeed, the Wilde scandal and its attendant publicity, by outraging not only sexual, but also social and monetary, taboos (Wilde was a free spender), was largely responsible, by way of inducing a reaction, for that ban on tenderness between males which was so marked a feature of the early-twentieth-century social scene, and which Forster so brilliantly pokes fun at in his novels. Fear of the body is always both cause and result of what he calls 'the undeveloped heart'.

On the other hand, the period of his early novels is also that of the beginnings of female emancipation. Although he was to portray few women who live lives of their own, Forster was among the early radical critics of that focus of Victorian morality, the family. Yet, even so, his innate caution and conservatism, perhaps his very bachelordom, prevented him from writing on the subject of the 'New Woman' with the immediacy of Wells in *Ann Veronica* (1909) or Dorothy Richardson in *Pilgrimage* (1915–38). We do not, for instance, find in his novels the sex warfare which was to break out in the suffragette movement, and which at the time they were being published was beginning to call for political equality by venting the stored-up repressions of the past fifty years with demonstrations, window-breaking and arson. (In 1913 a suffragette set fire to St Anne's Church, Eastbourne.) It seems rather a waste of Harriet Herriton that Forster did not write about them.

It was the emancipation of women, and the break-up of the family that this represented, which perhaps more than anything else smashed the dominance of Victorian religious morality. Butler's *The Way of All Flesh,* published posthumously in 1902, was a novel which Forster much admired, and it attacked both parental authority and contemporary religion. Forster would have written a study of its author had not the First World War prevented him. Butler was indeed one of his heroes: with his mordant wit and disrespectful clarity of mind he represented a positive attitude to contemporary change which offset Forster's innate caution. For, if a humanist could, as Hardy did, despair of adapting his nature to his environment, he might yet hope to adapt his environment to his nature. Civilisation could resolve itself into the science of power.

Forster distrusted power, and never sought it for himself: in this his spirit runs counter to the times, then as now. For in the early twentieth century the mastery of nature was apparently assured: the only thing left for men to fear was themselves. It was the object of humanist writers inspired by George Meredith, then enjoying a belated vogue, to reveal to their readers the underlying world of physical reality which periodically rises to trap them into recognising their true natures, a process of comic judgement which we find at work not only in the plays of Shaw (who had greeted Meredith's *Essay on Comedy* with enthusiasm) but in Forster's early novels as well. But in them the smugness attendant on the Meredithian attitude is itself a target for his mockery.

Forster was writing as one of what may be called the radical élite. Its analysis of what was wrong with the society of its day was based on an impatience with what it saw as the muddle and stagnation of lower-class life, the complacent philistinism of the bourgeoisie, and the vested interests of the well-to-do. The mass thinking which accompanied mass production was (thanks to the enormous popularity of Harmsworth's *Daily Mail*) largely right-wing in tendency. The real radicals belonged mostly to the upper middle class, which was where Forster was in contact with them. Sidney and Beatrice Webb exemplify this group, with their relentless logic, materialism and essentially paternalistic benevolence. But this world was not Forster's, as the biography of Lowes Dickinson would show.

For Forster, in his determined individualism, his combination of unorthodoxy in the inner life with social conformity of an ironically accepting kind, was to some extent a Victorian. While responsive to the enormous surge of social change going on around him, and emancipated in his plainness of speech and determination not to be hurried into merely fashionable activities, he lived strongly from his inner world of imagination.

William Plomer has observed how Forster treated his friends as characters in a novel 'and himself living, as in a novel, in a network of relationships with them'.[5] He did not self-consciously stand outside his own life, though he understood its circumstances very well, and could write essays of a sociological cast with illuminating grace; and he recognised what progressive writers tend to forget: that the movement of human history, as recorded in the consciousness of its participants, is slower than intellectuals like to think. Thus, where the lives of the bourgeoisie were concerned, the Victorian age lingered on into the Edwardian, and the Edwardian age in its turn could still be sensed in the provinces until the Second World War. Until then the middle class were still firmly in possession of the national ethos, continuing to live in Eastbourne, but in rather smaller houses and with rather smaller families. Their sons and daughters attended schools like Forster's Kent House; the boys in time would go on to Eastbourne College. If family prayers came to an end, and the majority of church-goers became 'four-wheelers' (to employ a clerical jocosity), only attending in a perambulator, a wedding carriage or a hearse, formal manners still prevailed, a show of cultured activity was maintained, and above all everyone knew their social place: for Eastbourne (or Tunbridge Wells or Weybridge) read Sawston. The Victorian Compromise may have been dead by the time that Forster wrote *A Passage to India,* but the people who were conditioned by it still survived, drawing their dividends like the Schlegel sisters and Aunt Juley, and following a certain prescribed standard of outlook and morals. It took the Second World War to upset their position of unassuming, unexciting supremacy; but even so it is an ironic fact that, when German bombs fell on Eastbourne, the Free Library, Technical Institute and three of the churches were demolished, but the College survived, the symbol of a basic imperturbability that had none the less forfeited its warrant in a strong, uncompromising *Raj.*

Forster's novels, therefore, whatever qualities they may have in common with Jane Austen's, did not grow out of a settled world like hers. They do not present us with the sense of a stable society of achieved power, as do those of Henry James, nor one of steady if unimaginative purpose, like those of Wells or Arnold Bennett. But they are conservative in their manner of rendering their setting, especially when we compare them with those of

D. H. Lawrence, while their authorial interpolations and reliance upon plot set them apart from the work of such writers as Ford Madox Ford and Virginia Woolf. As to influences, they are few and most elusive – Butler? Proust? The latter can have affected only *A Passage to India*. No, Forster was imaginatively an original. Hardy perhaps is his nearest source; he wrote that 'the work of Hardy is my home'.[6] The real influence upon him, however, was not literary but historical, the changes and upheavals, the questionings and tensions of the three decades in which he grew up and became a novelist. And he viewed those changes and upheavals, and absorbed them into his inner life, less perhaps from the standpoint of a visionary with his gaze on the eternal and unseen than from that of one who was attached to small, intimate, unpretentious places such as Rooksnest, and who refused to reject the social world in which he lived, even while he could see the danger to himself in not doing so. It is an artistic heroism of an unusual and, to the morally rigorous, of a most perplexing kind.

3   Biographies and Criticism

Forster's writing was always closely related to his own time.
Once certain youthful immaturities have been put behind, there
is little development in his output, at any rate in terms of change:
what we do find is a deepening and strengthening of concern, a
wisdom that grows out of the earlier sharpness and frivolities in
perfect continuity. (The frivolities, for better or worse, are never
quite left behind.) Common to all his fiction is the theme of
revelation, calling, judgement, salvation: although himself an
unbeliever, Forster still worked in the psychological framework
of the Christian myth. Because of this continuing preoccupation
the later books throw light retrospectively upon the earlier ones;
and the two biographies especially are significant for an understanding of the peculiar balance in his work between protest and
conformity, visionary insight and common sense. While pursu-
ing his ideals single-mindedly, he never disowned his origins or
background. Both books are works of piety, and throw almost as
much light upon their author as they do upon their subjects.

Goldsworthy Lowes Dickinson, indeed, is, in Brander's
phrase, 'rather like a twentieth-century prose Lycidas'.[1] But,
although a good biography, it is not quite the masterpiece that
W. H. Auden made it out to be.[2] By omitting (inevitably at the
time – 1934) any mention of its subject's homosexuality, it fails
to conform to the exhaustive standards demanded nowadays;
nor indeed did it meet Forster's own. He was to cite H. B.
Wortham's biography of Oscar Browning as 'one of the best
biographies of the last few years – quite unsparing and completely sympathetic'; but in *Goldsworthy Lowes Dickinson* sympathy is more apparent than unsparingness. Forster, however,
would probably have claimed that there was little to be unsparing about. He gives us the portrait of a good man who did good

24

unobtrusively, who worked selflessly for international peace and understanding, and who represented for him the very best that Cambridge had to offer. Cambridge itself figures largely in the book: even more than in *The Longest Journey* and *Maurice* does Forster stress its idyllic qualities.

Body and spirit, reason and emotion, work and play, architecture and scenery, laughter and seriousness, life and art – these pairs which are elsewhere contrasted were there fused into one. People and books reinforced one another, intelligence joined hands with affection, speculation became a passion, and discussion was made profound by love.   (Ch. 6)

The very cadences of the prose mirror the Forsterian version of the 'great good place'.

The triumph of the book lies in the way in which it reveals an outwardly uneventful life as significant and rich; and its attractiveness is increased by the innumerable characteristic small asides which pepper the text. Admittedly some of these are trivial, and to certain sensibilities vexing: 'when Labour gets thoroughly respectable, and is stimulated neither by danger nor by art, it does seem to acquire a sausage-and-mashed quality unknown to suburbia' (Ch. 9). But other comments are profound, and thrown off in that characteristically casual manner that only adds to the effect: thus, commenting on Dickinson's hatred of brutality and bullying, Forster remarks that 'his objection to rowdiness was not its noise but its inability to flourish without a victim'. The author and his subject are perfectly identified in that remark.

Indeed, the book is almost as much a portrait of Forster as it is of Dickinson: it portrays an ideal by which he lived and to which he aspired. It certainly sheds light on his literary sources. Dickinson had been one of his companions on his first visit to India in 1913; and the account of their voyage out is vintage Forster, in its verve, apparent inconsequence and intellectual sparkle.

We hated the boat, but the voyage to Bombay was fascinating. I have been that way since, but have never again seen such colours in the sea, so many flying fish, dolphins and sharks, such sunsets, such flights of birds and of butterflies (the last-named meeting us when we were still two days from the Indian coast). On board were many Anglo-Indians, as they were then called. These I have often seen again. The contrast between their clan and our clique was amusing. We were dubbed 'The Professors' or 'The Salon', and there was the same little nip of frost in these jests as in the title of 'The Three Graces' which had been fastened on Dickinson and his school friends at Charterhouse. They recognized that we were gentlemen, sahibs even, yet there was a barrier. No doubt we did look queer, and once when we were all four in a row at our tea a young officer opposite could not keep grave.   (Ch. 11)

That last phrase, a blend of Max Beerbohm and Beatrix Potter, is characteristic; but so also is the way he relates the experience back to Dickinson's schooldays, and his understanding of the situation in terms of inherited attitudes and conditioned reflexes: Forster often portrays his social types in almost puppet-like terms.

The pace of the passage then accelerates:

We played chess on Sundays, compared Dostoyevsky with Tolstoy publicly, argued over the shape of the Earth at the breakfast-table, balanced on bollards instead of playing deck-games, and discovered another young officer, a very different one, Kenneth Searight, who pursued romance and poetry in a solitary deckchair. We kept diaries. 'The extent of the heat may be judged from the fact that, on descending to my cabin, a tube of Kolynos was found in a semi-liquid condition' is a sentence which Dickinson gave me to put in mine. He said it was the ideal diarist style.

Most authors would have stopped at this point, content to have transcribed a humorous passage with a neat dry wit; but the reflective man in Forster was too strong to leave matters there.

I transcribe it here not for that reason but because nonsense is too seldom recorded. Wit and humour get put into a biography, foolery is missed out. It is so evanescent, it needs a gesture or a smile to fix it, and these cannot be transcribed. Dickinson could be ever so gay and ridiculous, laughing and talking at once, making everyone laugh, shooting out little glints of nonsense like flying fish.

With those fish we have come full circle to where the account began. Touches like this give one the sense of an experience completely apprehended and absorbed.

Dickinson's observations did more than transfer themselves to Forster's diary. Here, for instance, are Mrs Callendar and Mrs Turton all ready for *A Passage to India*;

> Anglo-Indian society is the devil – it's worse than America. We eschew it all we can. It's the women more than the men that are at fault. There they are, without their children, with no duties, no charities, with empty minds and hearts, trying to fill them by playing tennis and despising the natives. . . .

Not only this comment, but also what prompted it, was put to use. Elsewhere Forster criticises Dickinson's attitude to India as too pessimistic, while at the same time allowing that his conclusions were in part conditioned by his temperament. One feels that even in the biography a dialogue with his friend is going on. 'It was a revelation to him that men could take such constant and passionate interest in the unseen, and less of a revelation that neither their conduct nor their art seemed to benefit thereby.' A sentence like that makes one appreciate what a finely distinguishing cast of mind Forster brought to his examination of Anglo-Indian affairs.

The account in *A Passage to India* of the sequel to the Marabar expedition, while it accurately reflects the aftermath of the Amritsar massacre, was influenced by Dickinson's attitude to the Great War. His pacifism matches the attempt of Cyril Fielding, the man of moderation in that novel, to keep his head while all around were losing theirs. 'He was condemned to follow the intellect in a world that had become emotional.' Dickinson's moderation and intelligence were to be powerful influences in Forster's development; but Forster's response to them was not static, and he was to re-examine them in the Second World War.

Indeed, in undertaking the Life of Dickinson, Forster was not only paying a personal tribute to a man he loved and revered: he was also expounding indirectly the liberal ideals which he was to carry with him to the grave. They were not to be associated merely (if 'merely' be not too easily dismissive a word) with the foundering fortunes of the Liberal Party: rather they consisted of an ideal of individual behaviour that owed as much to Walter Pater and the Aesthetic movement as to the *Principia Ethica* of G. E. Moore. Forster never read this book, which appeared a year after he went down from Cambridge, and in the Dickinson biography he even gets the date of publication wrong; but Moore's ideas were the intellectual air he breathed, and were what put him in sympathy with his Bloomsbury friends, with whom his name has otherwise been too readily associated. What he gained from Moore's influence was a sense of personal priorities, the belief that individual experience was uniquely precious and that a man had a responsibility to his own mode of consciousness. Thus he writes of Dickinson that

> he dreaded the increasing rush and fuss of university business, not for selfish reasons but because it tended to neglect the needs of the individual undergraduate and to keep him in the position of a child, children being more easily managed. And he mistrusted research even more, although it is in itself so admirable and so necessary, because research atrophies the mind and renders it incapable of human intercourse. . . . (Ch. 10)

Forster himself endorses this view, both here and in his attitude to literary criticism, evident in *Aspects of the Novel* and elsewhere; but he has his reservations, going on to comment that

> There is a third Cambridge whose existence he forgot – the agglomeration conveniently known as 'the varsity' which takes pass-degrees, roars round football fields, sits down in the middle of Hammersmith Broadway after the boat race, and covers actresses with soot. Silly and idle young men did not come his way, no more did hearties and toughs unless they had intellectual leanings.

Forster himself was never abstracted from society in that way, and his friendships with non-academic people reveal a mental wholeness that complements the emotional resolution that it involved.

II

Of all the fictional characters that Forster was to create, the one with whom he appears to have identified most completely at an intellectual level is a woman, Margaret Schlegel in *Howards End*. In her he embodies his dialogue with the personal idealism and aesthetic morality of Lowes Dickinson; and her search for the proper balance between material and spiritual realities is Forster's own. It was in keeping with this sense of 'Only connect' that he should towards the end of his life have turned to the writing of the life of his great-aunt Marianne. This involved him in an exploration of spiritual values from the angle of a religious tradition that excluded the numinous. That he was himself affected by it may be deduced from the uncertainty with which, in the Life of Dickinson, he appears to handle a subtle case of spiritual materialism on his subject's part. 'He hoped for a small circle of light which science would gradually enlarge; beyond this circle stretches a region which, so long as it is unconquered, belongs to imagination and poetry' (Ch. 7). There is no indication that Forster himself realises that this scale of measurement, one which reserves the numinous for a department which the material cannot touch, is in fact that very attitude to spirituality which his fiction so forcefully rejects. The scale of measurement, one in terms of conquest and delimitation, is in fact a Wilcoxian scale. Forster's apparent inability to perceive this distinction prevents him from relating Dickinson's ethical attitudes to his own more visionary experience. (The latter term refers to his experience as a writer, rather than to any personal mystical experience he may have had. It would appear, from such records as we possess, that he had none.)

In writing of Dickinson, Forster was writing of a man who did in many respects constitute an ideal; but in writing of his great-aunt he was taking another look at a world whose values his younger self had needed to reject. Perhaps for this very reason *Marianne Thornton* is the more lively and original book of the two, certainly the one which is more likely to be read with enjoyment by later generations. It is, as he says, a domestic biography; but while full of intimacy and charm it opens out to become a piece of genuine social history. Forster's analysis of his great-aunt's eighteenth-century background is clear and sympathetic: his interpretation of family quarrels and domestic upheavals as being indicative of wider issues is the method that he had employed in his novels. This book is indeed very close to his fictional world: it speaks the same kind of language, being written in a relaxed, self-confident manner, generous, humorous, occasionally tart. Not tart enough, however, for some critics: Graham Hough, for instance, reviewing the book in *The Spectator,* claimed that, 'for once, his tone is less than impeccable; it seems to suggest a partial reconciliation with that high-minded communal bullying which it was formerly his main business to reject'.³ But Forster's affection is reserved for the late Victorian virtues of dedication, modesty and loyalty; what anger there is left in him is directed against the intolerance of sexual nonconformity. Moreover, his critique of Victorian emotionalism is balanced by his dislike of the twentieth century's lack of it. Thus he can write of his great-grandfather's proposal of marriage that 'it can be best understood by readers who tolerate an outmoded approach to love'. (That 'tolerate' is extremely telling.) Equally balanced is his account of the mourning following his great-grandmother's death.

> Then sorrow broke out again with accumulated force. To convey it is difficult – not through lack of material but through superabundance. The bereaved and their comforters all write enormous letters, symptoms are dwelt on, dying speeches and death-moments repeated and extended, the Will of God is bowed to again and again, sorrow is so persistently exhibited as joy that both become meaningless.

The tone of this seems about to turn into the patronising mockery of Lytton Strachey's *Eminent Victorians*; but Forster, as always, is anxious to mediate between one age and another. So he proceeds,

> The twentieth-century observer has to remind himself that inside all this cocoonery of words there was love, there was pain. It was the technique of the age and of a section of the middle class; it lasted, as far as my own family were concerned, into the 1850s. After that the technique of mourning shortens, it is now very brief and some sensible people cut out mourning altogether. With it they cut down pain, which has

practical advantages, and with pain they cut down love.
People today love each other from moment to moment as much
as ever their ancestors did, but loyalty of soul, such as the
elder Thorntons possessed, is on the decrease.

('The Death Beds')

The criticism here goes deep; but its quietness of tone, its
awareness of alternatives, stops it from being self-righteous or
sentimental. And the transition from the homely 'People today
love each other from moment to moment' to the phrase about
'loyalty of soul' is essentially Forsterian in its move from simplicity to instinctive dignity. It is this kind of progression which
renders his moral arguments so persuasive.

One of the peculiar interests of *Marianne Thornton* is that it
shows so much of the ancestry not only of the author but also of
that 'Sawston' world with which he had such a complex relationship. The ties which bound him to it were extremely close.
Nevertheless the account of his boyhood which closes the book is
markedly free from sentimental nostalgia. Much as he loved
Rooksnest, he had a just appreciation of what it did for him. It
gave him 'a slant upon society and history. It is a middle-class
slant, atavistic, derived from the Thorntons, and it has been
corrected by contact with friends who have never had a home in
the Thornton sense, and do not want one' ('My Recollections').

The fact that there is no qualifying statement following that
declaration is typical of him. What concerned him about his
childhood was that it had given him an understanding of how his
ancestors had felt about Battersea Rise. The spoliation of the
area after the house's demolition calls forth a piece of prose to
match his earlier account of the growth of the New Town of
Stevenage and, in his fourth novel, of the threat of London to the
rural landscape round Howards End. Throughout his work we
find a nostalgic sense of place, evidenced in his loving descriptions of houses seen less as architecture than as homes. Again,
Howards End, his condition-of-England novel, provides the
most eloquent examples.

Indeed *Marianne Thornton* is a kind of retrospective source-
book for much that we find in *Howards End*. Forster's appreciation of and reservations about his great-aunt's social philanthropy and charitable activities illuminate issues that are discussed in the earlier book. He notes that her desire to educate the

poor 'combines, in varying degrees, with the desire for a good
supply of servants'. 'She conceived of society as an agglomera-
tion of homes and of helpers in the home. She had little perception of the industrialism that was rapidly engulfing both girls
and boys . . .' ('Educational').

The Schlegel sisters could do better than this; but, just as they
are representative of the world into which the young Morgan
was to escape, so also it is characteristic of him that he should not
exempt that world from the kind of critical enquiry which was
more readily turned upon the world which he had left. And in
any case it is clear that his own brand of humanism was in part
derived from his great-aunt's. Of the two motives he ascribes to
her zeal for education, the first was one which he himself could
share, 'her dislike of ignorance and her eighteenth-century faith
in reason'. But he is fully aware of

> the weakness in the Thornton–Wilberforce outlook – the
> weakness that has been mercilessly exposed by the Ham-
> monds and other critics. . . . When the slavery was industrial
> they did nothing and had no thought of doing anything; they
> regarded it as something 'natural', to encounter it was an
> educational experience, and an opportunity for smug thank-
> fulness. Misery might be alleviated at the soup kitchen level,
> but to do more might make the workers unruly and even
> unchristian.

This is sharp, incisive and by present standards orthodox: we all
talk about 'society' now. But Forster refuses to lose human
contact with his ancestors. It is no surprise, therefore, when he
follows the above words with this comment:

> I agree with the above line of criticism. But I do not share the
> moral indignation that sometimes accompanies it. The really
> bad people, it seems to me, are those who do no good any-
> where and help no one either at home or abroad. There are
> plenty of them about, and when they are clever as well as
> selfish they often manage to slip through their lives unnoticed,
> and so escape the censure of historians.
>
> ('On Clapham Common')

The clipped sentences serve to reinforce the point of his observation.

But *Marianne Thornton* is above all a personal book, a companionable book in which we are taken gently into Forster's confidence, and full of dry asides which subtly compliment us by putting us on a footing with the author himself. This shared point of view enables Forster to make use of evidence in a discriminating manner peculiarly his own. His account of his great-uncle's elopement to the cõntinent with his sister-in-law is mediated through a letter from a gossiping female relation who witnessed the couple's departure from Dover.

> The following letter . . . has an earthiness – or should one say a saltiness? – about it which is a welcome relief after so much high-mindedness, fair-mindedness, discrimination and recrimination. Here is exactly what we want, namely an ordinary woman on the gape.   ('Deceased Wife's Sister')

The good humour of that last remark is irresistible. It is a perfect example of the imaginative common sense which makes *Marianne Thornton* such a satisfying conclusion to the author's literary career.

III

The ease and naturalness of the book were qualities that Forster had acquired over fifty years of journalism and occasional writings; his simplicity of approach had also been furthered, not always beneficially, by his teaching at the Working Men's College. But one can trace an evolution from the tiresomely arch mandarin style of his earlier essays in *Pharos and Pharillon* and *Abinger Harvest* into the firm outspokenness of the later pieces collected in *Two Cheers for Democracy* (a title itself perhaps conditioned by his informal teaching career). The difference between the collections is quite remarkable: the contents of the first are frequently self-conscious and belles-lettrist; the third is a coherent, outspoken book in its own right.

Unlike Lawrence, Virginia Woolf or Katherine Mansfield, Forster could not make out of a review a lively piece of explorative literary criticism. Indeed, writing, as such, seems to have meant comparatively little to him, excellently though he usually wrote himself, and despite the fact that the craft and discipline involved in it clearly brought fulfilment to his residual puritanism. No more than in religion or political action would he submit himself or his liberty of thought and action to the business of being a professional writer.

Thus, even *Aspects of the Novel* commences (following a characteristic tribute to the founder of the Clark Lectures) with a rebuttal of the historical method of study. It is true that as a practising novelist himself Forster probably disliked the way in which literary critics so readily ascribe influences and precedents when writing about their chosen authors; but in this case his refusal to talk about influences was because, he maintains, only the genuine scholar can use them with honesty. Though pseudo-scholarship may be, at its best, 'the homage paid by ignorance to learning', it is not equipped to speak of influences with any real base in fact, remaining therefore a higher guessing game. Forster accordingly (if modestly) sets his novelists in an eternal present. For, as he goes on to observe, the novel is concerned not just with life in time but with the life of values as well – with what might be called linear time and vertical time, that dual mode of awareness which informs his own work. So, too, he distinguishes between *homo sapiens* and *homo fictus.* We can know people in fiction as we never can in life.

What does emerge clearly from *Aspects of the Novel* is the essentially musical nature of his inspiration; and this has its importance, in aesthetic terms, with regard to the liberal ethic. Most Edwardian fiction appears to be sculptured, or, in lesser instances, assembled: novels were, as we say nowadays, 'packaged'. 'Workmanlike' is an appropriate adjective, one that Arnold Bennett would have accepted, and which he and so many half-forgotten contemporaries duly earned. But this kind of novel witnessed to a petrification: certainly it consorted well with an ethical and aesthetic ideal centred in notions of willpower, self-control, and a sense of purpose – that of the Victorian businessman, in fact. Henry James and Joseph Conrad had substituted for this conception the idea of organic growth; the seed or germ or, in Jamesian language, the *donnée* of the novel being nurtured by the writer into full, prolific flowering, to yield its maximum wealth of meaning. But even here the emphasis is on fullness of rendering, on an act achieved.

Forster's notion of what constitutes a novel is more elusive; he is less concerned with defining what a novel is than with elucidating what it does. His own ethical training, and what one may term his religious instincts, forbade him to make of writing an end in itself (though it must be added that the actual structure and patterning of his novels show them to be the products of an artistic conscience of an absolute and demanding kind). And it is clear that, for him, the significant elements in a novel are those moments of specific illumination which are the highlights in his own.

He was sceptical about the usefulness of criticism – especially, it would seem, where the novel was concerned. Certainly he was capable of making ruthlessly merry over academic solemnities in this field. Reviewing an American study of the novel in 1919, he declared that 'we learn, not from studying a book, but from enjoying it'[4] – and then pounces on the author for failing to realise that 'in consequence there is nothing to be learned from his'. And twenty-five years later he can say that 'The novel, in my view, has not any rules, and so there is no such thing as the art of fiction.' But this is to confuse art with prescription, and is a surprising lapse in one who normally is so sensitive to shades of meaning. To say that there is only the art of the individual novelist is not to dismiss the question; it is simply a refusal to proceed further. The truth of the matter would seem to be that Forster was not interested. He was dubious about the academic mind, and wrote in his commonplace book that 'The desire to appear weighty often disguises itself as disinterested curiosity.'[5] Disciplined methodology, alert commentaries, systematic rigour – these current desiderata are not to be found in his literary appreciations. Also, on his own admission, he was reacting against his immediate forebears, Meredith, Stevenson, Henry James, and all the talk about 'style' and 'form' that centered round them. He feels that the immediate past 'is like a stuffy room, and the succeeding generations waste their time in trying to tolerate it. All they can do is to go out leaving the door open behind them.'[6] Already there may be people who feel that way about his own work.

The cheerful free-wheeling of Forster's approach offers its own kind of challenge to the standards of today, especially at a time when the various critical schools mask so many different ideologies. But Forster belongs to a literary tradition that was not afraid to confess to personal preference. '. . . how rare, how precious is frivolity! How few writers can prostitute all their powers! They are always implying "I am capable of higher things."' Thus Forster on Ronald Firbank: what from a Robert Lynd or an E. V. Lucas would be a mere playful exclamation, from Forster is a dart aimed with precision. That he should write perceptively on Firbank, Forrest Reid and Howard Overing Sturgis is not surprising,[7] for these three very different novelists share in their several ways a homosexual sensibility, and he may thus be supposed to have a fellow feeling for them; but his intuitive, empathetic approach enables him to illustrate authors of a very different kind – Ibsen, T. E. Lawrence, Sinclair Lewis, Conrad, none of whose work bears much resemblance to his own. But on Jane Austen he disappoints. Mannered, a little prim, he is belles-lettrist in the worst sense. Charm is one of his greatest endowments, but here he uses it as a stock in trade with trivialising effect. All in all, the criticism is (inevitably, given its lack of method) hit or miss; though, unlike much critical writing more forcefully organised and organising, even when it misses it is still pleasurable to read. Significantly, in *Two Cheers for Democracy* the literary studies occupy less space, and are, with the exception of the long (and excellent) essays on John Skelton, George Crabbe and C. P. Cavafy, of a still more casual kind. And in the Rede Lecture on Virginia Woolf (1941) (which is a great improvement on the earlier essay reprinted in *Abinger Harvest*) the best points concern his subject's social rather than her literary attitudes. Thus:

> she handed out no bouquets to the middlemen who have arrogated to themselves the right of interpreting the crowd, and get paid for doing so in the daily press and on the wireless. These middlemen form after all a very small clique – larger than the Bloomsbury they so tirelessly denounce, but a mere drop in the ocean of humanity. And since it was a drop whose distinction was proportionate to its size she saw no reason to conciliate it.[8]

Those words continue to sound with a tart and wholesome timeliness.

Indeed, it is as a social commentator rather than as a literary critic that Forster himself excelled, nor was he ever tempted, as many are, to exchange the two roles to their mutual confusion.

His literary essays are retrospective, written by one who had learned what he could do, not by one who was still an apprentice. He is not a critic in the professional sense, but an artist and a reader: the literary essays are records of enthusiasms and enjoyment. They are similar in inspiration and technique to those of Virginia Woolf, and fall under the same condemnation in certain schools. But, even without a conscious theory, Forster was in fact seeking to record the movement and awareness of life which in their differing ways both Lawrence and Virginia Woolf were also aiming for. Lawrence wrote that 'The business of art is to reveal the relation between man and his circumambient universe, at the living moment';[9] and, although what Forster specifically deals with is 'the *eternal* moment', in doing so he organises his novels in a pattern of symbolism that implies a whole series of 'living moments' related to an overall design that, as art, has a permanent significance. The visionary moment or epiphany is for him a call to life, not merely an object of static contemplation; and his characters have to learn to realise it as such. In his final novel we are presented with what amounts to a 'dark' epiphany; but its implications are the same.

4 The Early Stories

I

The Fitzwilliam Museum at Cambridge used at one time to display a painting called *The Little Faun*.[1] A table is set beneath flowering cherry trees, and a small boy is standing on it, pulling at the branches. Beside him, also on the table, is the little faun: two young women are standing by, and one of them tweaks its tail. The faun parents, dim animal shapes, watch guardedly through leaves. It is a characteristic piece of Edwardian whimsy, full of shimmering pink and white; but a more knowing generation may detect tell-tale undertones. That domestication of the wild, that dainty sexual titillation, the breaking of taboo as the child stands upon the table – all these things add up to a distillation of the evasively erotic that typifies much writing of the period, an example of the Victorian compromise carried over into the field of sex awareness. 'Naughty but nice' – the coyness of Edwardian music-hall coquetry is an attempt to tame the beast, and an instance of that incurable English tendency to dissolve all uncomfortable realities in charm. It was a temptation to which Forster himself was not immune, and his early short stories in particular provide us with examples of his yielding to it. But, more importantly, they show us the way in which he rose above it, and thus sharpened his literary style so that it could undertake more far-reaching explorations in his novels. Instead of rejecting the feeble literary tradition outright, he worked his way through it to a fully mature comprehension of his own.

The tradition is summed up in J. M. Barrie's enormously popular *Peter Pan*, first produced in 1904, the same year that saw the appearance of Forster's 'The Story of a Panic'. The play combines ambivalence towards the adult world with a celebration of childhood for its own sake. By the time of Forster's early stories the literary cult of childhood was at its height: Kenneth Grahame's *The Golden Age* (1895) is a characteristic example,

38

and in it children live a life that by virtue of its greater spontaneity and naturalness is an implied rebuke to the adult world – the
conjoining of Pan with Peter was not surprising when it came.
But this tradition was very different from the radical insights of
Wordsworth or Blake: it had become a matter of nostalgia, an
alternative vision of reality, persuasive on its own terms merely,
and more suggestive of escape than transformation. Ultimately
it was the expression of a sense of guilt – as Henry James
unforgettably demonstrated in 'The Turn of the Screw', the
governess's 'adult' fear of corruption being the force that raises
the phantoms and thus injures, in one case fatally, the two
children. *Peter Pan* and the later *Mary Rose* (1920), Barrie's
logical conclusion of the tradition, would seem to suggest that it
is better not to grow up at all.

The fact that in *Peter Pan* the life of the fairy Tinker Bell is
made dependent on the audience's belief in her, though dramatically effective, also testifies to a sentimentalising subjectivity
where the supernatural is concerned: no self-respecting elemen-
tal of earlier traditions would have allowed itself to be exting-
uished by such disobliging schoolboys as might, when asked if
they believed in fairies, choose to bellow 'NO!' But the heyday of
imperial wealth and power was essentially materialistic in its
spirituality, a point that both Forster and Lawrence in their very
different ways were to make repeatedly. The immaterial in
whatever form was just that – of no real significance save as an
adornment, a 'civilising' extra, something *added* to the real ends
of life, which were money and power. Lawrence in his essay on
John Galsworthy unforgettably exposes and deflates this attitude, as he analyses the contemporary usage of the word
'passion'.[2] And Forster too, though less by denunciation than by
mockery, was to make a similar point. His story 'Other Kingdom' is a good example of it.

The short stories, indeed, though rightly accounted the least of
his fiction, are essential to any understanding of his imaginative
world. Written concurrently with the early novels, they provide,
as short stories tend to do, clear instances of authorial obsessions; and they thus highlight the novels, which put those
obsessions to more objective use. Revealing a tendency towards
violence and shock tactics, they are frequently playful, but as
cats are playful – with their claws. They are designed to discon-
cert, and witness to an imaginative impulse that is fundamental-

ly rebellious. But Forster was not by nature an aggressive man: the protest comes out in the shape of farce and fantasy. As Wilfred Stone observes, the stories 'record the first stage of a rebellion against school, church, and the intolerable chaperonage of loving parents and guardians'.[3] Fantasy is used by Forster as 'an unction for disobedience',[4] and by its means he breaks free from the domestic world which was constricting him. And yet even this statement is questionable, for in his hands fantasy returns us to the life which had occasioned it. Forster is not a fantasist of the mythological kind; he does not create new worlds. A feeling for the supernatural was useful to him as a literary device; it was a means of saying something else, never an end in itself. Its appearance in the various short stories he wrote between the early 'Lucy' fragments and *Maurice* illustrates his treatment of so-called 'reality' in these books, and points to the existence of a kind of imaginative overworld to which he regularly returned. It was out of its elements that the novels were to grow.

In *The Longest Journey* he parodies, in the shape of Rickie Elliot's proposed collection 'Pan Pipes', the kind of tales he himself was writing. But at the same time he satirised the readership for which such stories were designed. Agnes's comment on one tale (which, ironically, Forster wrote himself, as 'Other Kingdom') helps us to place both it and her. 'Allegory. Man = modern civilization (in bad sense). Girl = getting into touch with nature.' The misunderstanding, the oversimplification, make the point. So does Stephen Wonham's reaction when he reads it. 'In touch with Nature! The girl was a tree!' The distinction is vital; and at the time in which these stories were being written it was consistently confused. Forster was attempting to liberate himself from a bad literary tradition.

Indeed, the trivialisation of supernatural themes has been a steady and inevitable process coincident with the growth of materialist philosophies since the seventeenth century. One can trace it in the decline of the *Longaevi* of medieval cosmology through the more playful diminutive fairies of Shakespeare and Drayton to those vestigial presences, half-assumed into classical mythology, that we find in Milton. Victorian fantasy provided a further source for the tradition when such an influential writer as George Macdonald made use of German folklore and philosophy. It is significant that in Macdonald's stories the instruments of redemption are quasi-maternal figures: the Great-Great-Grandmother (fourfold maternal) in *The Princess and the Goblin* (1873) comes readily to mind. But no less prominent in Macdonald's fiction are corrective 'aunt' figures, such as the wise woman in *The Lost Princess* (1875), the successors of such better-known disciplinarians as Mrs Be-Done-By-As-You-Did in Charles Kingsley's *The Water Babies* (1863). In Victorian fantasy the woman plays a dominating role; and it is the more significant that Forster, much encumbered with women in his early life, should in his own fantasies turn instead to the young male or brother figure as his deliverer. And the deliverer is frequently light-hearted. The stories are notably lacking in solemnity or, to use a word much in use in the period, 'wonder'.

Nor do they bear much relation to that other aspect of late-nineteenth-century fantasy, the ghost story. The malign aspects of the supernatural evoked by Sheridan Le Fanu or M. R. James are nowhere to be found in Forster's work, though James was in his heyday at the time these tales were being written; nor was Forster himself influenced by the very different, but equally compelling, use of the paranormal to be found in the novels of Henry James and Dickens. The subconscious fears and bogeys on which all these writers play are absent from his work: they are replaced by high spirits, a caustic wit and a rebellious impishness. And this is interesting in view of the fact that much of this macabre writing was done by bookish unmarried men with dominating maternal influences, men such as the three Benson brothers – or, for that matter, Henry James himself. Forster was perhaps more emancipated than has sometimes been allowed.

The figure of Pan appears a good deal in his early writing, as it does in that of many of his contemporaries. Max Beerbohm's 'Maltby and Braxton' makes merry play with the fashion.

> From the time of Nathaniel Hawthorne to the outbreak of the War, current literature did not suffer from any lack of fauns. . . . We had not yet tired of them and their hoofs and their slanting eyes and their way of coming suddenly out of woods to wean quiet English villages from respectability. We did tire later.[5]

In this respect it is worthwhile to compare Forster's work with that of two writers whom Beerbohm would have had in mind, Arthur Machen and H. H. Munro, better known as Saki. Machen had first made his name with the (then) luridly sensational novella *The Great God Pan* (1894), in which sexual energies are portrayed as obscene and retrogressive. In time he came to dislike the book, which had pandered all too successfully to contemporary tastes in the occult, and in *The Hill of Dreams* (1907) he produced a novel of genuine visionary power which, in its positive stresses, highlights Forster's work. It represents the quintessence of Machen's imaginative world: a solitary boy growing up in a landscape which both fascinates and scares him; the surrounding enclave of adult obtuseness and conventionality; intimations of an ancient civilisation among the ruins of Roman Caerleon; and, most significantly, the dawning of sexuality during sleep on the summit of an ancient earthwork. But the conflict between the physical and imaginative sides of Lucian's nature results in his self-destruction among the arid terraces of London suburbia. The power of Pan is destructive when the human spirit is unable to contain it: the theme of *The Bacchae* is the theme of much literature of this period. The peculiar distinction of Machen's achievement lies in its evocation of an urban landscape that is seen, through the transfiguring vision, as being no less open to spiritual powers and forces than the wild romantic one of Gwent: there is no imaginative departmentalism in his work. Nonetheless he is unable to envisage any reconciliation between the two realities: the prose and the passion will not connect, and in such a later work as *The Secret Glory* (published in 1922 but written fourteen years earlier) the disconnection leads to a breakdown even of the structure of the book itself.

The quest for a transfigured universe, the poetic insight hailed in Machen's literary manifesto *Hieroglyphics* (1902) as being the life of all genuine literature, is to be found in Forster's early work as well. But in Forster the expression of this feeling is tempered by a sharpness of tone that is closer to that of another minor but vitalising writer of the period, Saki. Most of Saki's tales are social satires of varying degrees of frivolity and anger; but one or two are concerned with the operations of the supernatural, usually in the forms of animal malignity. Pan here is the avenger: Saki, a homosexual and, like Forster, brought up by women (in this case a most dire pair of aunts) frequently depicts the female put to rout, whether in jest, as in 'The Boar-Pig', or in deadly earnest, as in 'Shredni Vashtar' or 'The Music on the Hill'. In the latter story the victim of Pan's destructive power is one of those shallow society women who people many of the author's lighter tales; in the former it is yet another aunt. The hostility of the animal world – also portrayed effectively in Machen's short novel *The Terror* (1917) – is one which Saki appears to endorse, especially in view of the more ribald treatment of such avenging creatures as the cat Tobermory. His intentions, however, seem ambiguous. One notes that his hero-figure Bassington bears the demonic name of Comus; the disruptive Clovis, on the other hand, is surnamed Sangrail. In Saki's world, destruction and dislocation contain elements of deliverance.

II

When compared with the stories of Machen and Saki, those of Forster seem rather tame; but, although more obviously didactic than the other two, he writes with a deeper and more wide-ranging purpose. Five of his stories are tales of Pan, and the production of all but one of them parallels the writing of his early novels. They deal with possession; but, unlike Machen, Forster shows himself to be as interested in its social consequences as he is in the condition of the possessed themselves.

In 'Albergo Empedocle' the unimaginative but honest Harold (sterling Anglo-Saxon name) falls asleep in a ruined Sicilian temple, and wakes in the knowledge that he has lived before. For him it is the quality of life – 'I was a lot greater than I am now' – which is important; but his 'cultured' fiancée[6] interprets this to mean that he has been a king, and she then, sentimentally, tries to fool herself that she likewise has lived before. But Harold will have none of this: the experience is not for romanticising. He alienates her; and the result is his own despair and gradual withdrawal into the past and into noncommunication. He is consigned to an asylum. The story is funny, sad, and alive with intelligence, compassion and wit. The supernatural theme has been made a vehicle for comment on the outlook of the pseudo-culture of the tourist mentality and on the alienating effects of a socially rigid and imaginatively limited way of life. Harold, first of Forster's athletes, is also the first of his victims. The visitation itself is ambiguous, for its destructive nature is really the result of the rest of the party's rejection of it. Tommy, the narrator, who is Harold's friend, remarks at the end that 'the greater has replaced the less, and he is living the life he knew to be greater than the life he lived with us'. This is the expected 'civilised' response. But Tommy goes on to say that 'if things had happened otherwise he might be living that greater life among us, instead of among friends of two thousand years ago'. It is this which is the distinctively Forsterian touch, the tentative optimism, the concern with quality of life rather than with imaginative indulgence.

'Albergo Empedocle' foreshadows much that is to be part of the Forsterian universe: the parenthetical, allusive humour; the amiable inanities of the more gently conventional old lady; the sudden sharp comment; the shared observation as between friend and friend. The tale seems almost as much confided as told. Forster always avoids the spectacular: he prefers to use implication. But there is nothing fey about Harold's experience: this is, in one sense, an anti-romantic story. Regrettably, Forster did not think it good enough to publish in *The Celestial Omnibus,* for it is less vulnerable to criticism than some that he did include there.

'The Story of a Panic', however, can have no place among their number: it is one of the surest, most vigorous tales that Forster wrote. Nearly all the ingredients of his early novels are present in this account of the stampeding of a sedate picnic party by the power of Pan. Here are the middle-class conventionalists (Tunbridge Wells, as it were): the spinster sisters whose nephew Eustace is subjected to the visitation of the God; the sentimental aesthete Leyland; the Reverend Mr Sandbach, ancestor of other clerical guardians of the proprieties; and the narrator, Mr Tytler, a Mr Pembroke who talks with the voice of Mr Pooter. The exchanges between him and Leyland anticipate one of the themes of *Howards End.*

> 'All the poetry is going from Nature,' [Leyland] cried, 'her lakes and marshes are drained, her seas banked up, her forests cut down. Everywhere we see the vulgarity of desolation spreading.'
> I have had some experience of estates, and answered that cutting was very necessary for the health of the larger trees.

Besides, it was unreasonable to expect the proprietor to derive no income from his lands. (I)

The two sides are played off against each other and both found wanting.

The Italian characters are likewise to be met again later, most significantly the young waiter Gennaro. He is the ideal friend whose death is to be the price for the English boy's release, but who dies, in mordantly Forsterian fashion, still clasping the fee for his treachery. The transition from sharp social comedy to terror is effortlessly managed, partly because Forster's attention at the moment of the picnic party's flight is concentrated on the characters' reactions. They all reveal themselves appropriately; and it is the aesthete who is most frightened. He knows enough to realise what the onset of Pan can mean, but not enough to accept it. It is far harder for him to recover from it than it is for the unimaginative innocents. In this story, the supernatural element is subordinate to the truth which it conveys. The reader is made to think, not jump; but none the less it is (with the exception of *A Passage to India*) the only one of Forster's tales to produce a genuinely frightening effect. This happens when Eustace perceives the goat's hoofmarks in the mud and rolls in them 'as a dog rolls'. The brevity of this is immensely forceful, an economy of means which Forster was to develop further; we are persuaded that the violence is real. Here is no sentimental post-Meredithian awakening to the joys of nature: Forster's vision at this point is nearer to that of Machen. Gennaro dies while 'Signora Scafetti burst into screams at the sight of the dead body, and, far down the valley towards the sea, there still resounded the shouts and the laughter of the escaping boy.'

Eustace's escape is from – what? Home? 'Ladies'? Too small a bedroom? The tale has a general social relevance, powered by a more personal urge. Its weakness lies in those passages of would-be lyrical evocation when Forster uses the incantatory prose current among his contemporaries: Tytler's account of Eustace's speech is quite out of character.

He spoke first of night and the stars and planets above his head, of the swarms of fire-flies below him, of the invisible sea below the fire-flies, of the great rocks covered with anemones and shells that were slumbering in the invisible sea. He spoke of the rivers and waterfalls, of the ripening bunches of grapes, of the smoking cone of Vesuvius and the hidden fire-channels that made the smoke, of the myriads of lizards who were lying curled up in the crannies of the sultry earth, of the showers of white rose-leaves that were tangled in his hair. And then he spoke of the rain and the wind by which all things are changed, of the air through which all things live, and of the woods in which all things can be hidden.   (III)

The prose, though musical and skilfully orchestrated, is archaic: these are not the words of Tytler. And they are not really the words of Eustace either. If anyone's, they are the words of Leyland.

But the escaping boy remains to haunt much of Forster's succeeding fiction, like an ultimately friendly demon. (In *Howards End*, however, and *A Passage to India*, Demeter and the Great Mother make their presence felt.) A substitution is effected: Eustace in one sense here *becomes* Gennaro, the 'clumsy, impertinent fisher lad', who is the one person who understands what has happened. And Gennaro is to be reborn as Gino Carella, as Stephen Wonham, as George Emerson, as Alec Scudder; and in each case he is to be bound up with, even to symbolise, a particular place (Monteriano, Wiltshire, Florence, the English woodland) which has significance for the novel's central consciousness, a significance extended into personal terms: 'for Forster, the raising of a single man to mythopoeic stature disguised and sublimated his homosexual passions'.[7] Certainly a sense of *withheld* passion energises the various manifestations of the demon boy; and in the later novels his role tends to be destructive. In *Howards End* he is to be disguised, almost too effectively, as Leonard Bast; and it is he, on one reading, who attacks Miss Quested in the Marabar cave. He can reduce the conventional and repressed, the muddled spiritual materialists, to 'panic and emptiness': Forster anticipates that phrase in this early tale. Here Eustace is liberated by force, and the cost is the destruction of his personality. The later fictions work towards a more positive outcome; and the distinction between compromise and balance is one which will concern Forster repeatedly from now on. Possession is not enough.

The two other Pan stories of the early period show the author's Edwardian side in more complete control. Of these 'The Curate's

Friend' is particularly revealing. The tale is about compromise; but it is itself a compromised production. The curate, whose sight of the faun enables him to bear the loss of his fiancée to another – tiresomely called 'the little friend' – lives on in the knowledge of what underlies reality; but he none the less stays part of that reality.

> And though I try to communicate that joy to others . . . and though I sometimes succeed, yet I can tell no one exactly how it came to me. For if I breathed one word of that, my present life, so agreeable and profitable, would come to an end, my congregation would depart, and so should I, and instead of being an asset to my parish, I might find myself an expense to the nation.

The irony enunciates the author's own situation as well as constituting his particular slant of vision. The closing words indeed, might serve him for an epigraph.

> Therefore in place of the lyrical and rhetorical treatment, so suitable to the subject, so congenial to my profession, I have been forced to use the unworthy medium of a narrative, and to delude you by declaring that this is a short story, suitable for reading in the train.

But this is a dangerous game to play; and this story in particular suffers from an ambiguity of approach. There is something of Harold Skimpole about the curate. He wants to have things both ways. Moreover, the actual presentation of the faun's arrival is arch, and the dialogue when the curate finds 'the little friend' and Emily embracing is pure fustian – or, if it is not, then it is parody such as gives the game away altogether: 'It is idle to chide. What should you know poor clerical creature, of the mystery of love of the eternal man and the eternal woman, of the self-effectuation of a soul?' This sort of thing collides not only with the narrator's tone, but also with the glimpse of 'the great pagan figure of the Faun' towering 'insolently' above them. And the final message of the faun is too slight (though it is telling) for what has gone before: 'To the end of your life you will swear when you are cross and laugh when you are happy.' This is, of course, a Forsterian ideal; but this kind of tale is not the best way of putting it across.

It may contain a homosexual reference (to quote Wilfred Stone,
'The story . . . is a covert love poem, and the spirit of that love is
illicit'⁸) but this does not affect its value.

'Other Kingdom' is more successful, partly because it is more
like a novel in miniature. The comedy is distinctively Edwardian: we are in the familiar world of the Herritons and the
Honeychurches. Harcourt Worters is a male surrounded by
sycophantic women, and rendered by them pompous and absurd
and thus, on Forster's reckoning, dangerous. (When, in a fit of
'playful' jealousy, he pinches his young nephew's leg, he draws
blood.) He is a spiritual materialist who seeks to buy and possess
what is intangible – in this case Other Kingdom Wood – as a
present to his fiancée, Evelyn Beaumont. Evelyn anticipates
Helen Schlegel with her protests against the world of 'rights' and
'apologies' and 'Society' and 'position'; she even anticipates,
albeit somewhat drastically, Helen's pastoral solution of her
dilemma: she turns into a dryad. Mr Worters is a typically
Forsterian Apollo, strangely pathetic as he tries to secure what it
will never be his to hold. And he is a perfect specimen of the
pseudo-aesthete. Speaking of the classics, he says,

> 'They were written before men began to really feel.' He
> coloured crimson. 'Hence, the chilliness of classical art – its
> lack of – of a something. Whereas later things – Dante – a
> Madonna of Raphael – some bars of Mendelssohn –' His voice
> trailed reverently away. We sat with our eyes on the ground,
> not liking to look at Miss Beaumont. It is a fairly open secret
> that she also lacks a something. She has not yet developed her
> soul.   (II)

It is a story narrated in Forster's most telling, thrifty manner,
though a little weighed down by its symbols. The names –
Worters, Ford, even Eve Beaumont (how conscious was that?) –
are offset by a more persuasive, Lawrentian type of description,
as when the narrator observes 'the pleasant, comfortable landscapes, full of cows and carriage horses out at grass, and civil
retainers'. But the tale relies too much on puns, as when Evelyn
fords the stream to the wood (Ford is the name of Mr Worters's
nephew, one of those sexually quelled young men who abound
piteously in Forster's fiction) while her lover follows her by way
of the bridge. And so it is with the 'supernatural' element: it

exists to point a moral, and is a product of the fancy rather than of the imagination. Evelyn's disappearance lacks the dramatic power of Eustace's flight: the demon boy here is not in evidence. As in all these early tales, 'The Story of a Panic' excepted, it is the young girl who goes free. Forster's frustrated compassion may be with the young men, but it is still a question for him of 'Ladies first'.

Ladies are much in evidence in what is in some ways a companion story, 'The Purple Envelope'. This, like 'Albergo Empedocle', was not included in *The Celestial Omnibus* collection.[9] It is Forster's one incursion into the macabre, and it forms an interesting gloss on 'Other Kingdom'. Once again we have a benevolent household despot surrounded by adoring females; but this time the nephew, Howard, is coarse-grained and triumphant.[10] In this tale pseudo-aestheticism is identified with dishonesty – the uncle has defrauded the nephew of his estate; while the outdoor scenes are far more robust and real than the sylvan glades of 'Other Kingdom'. There is much that is enigmatic about the story – for example, the identity of the middle-aged woman who brings Howard the oval-bored gun; but, since it is the healthy if brutalised reality of Howard's responses which the author seems to be commending, the enigmatic elements only contribute to our sense of the unreality of any attitude other than his. And an enigma is not the same thing as a muddle.

At one point in *A Passage to India* Mrs Moore remarks that 'I like mysteries but I rather dislike muddles.' 'The Story of the Siren' is an early tale which did not appear until 1920, when it was published by Leonard and Virginia Woolf at the Hogarth Press. It is certainly a mystery; and nowhere until *A Passage to India* was Forster to evoke so hauntingly the human sense of the supernatural. Once again we have a party – this time a boat-load – of tourists, who are confronted with the physical self-assurance and humility of the Italian. The loss beneath the waves of the narrator's notes on the Deist controversy is the appropriate prelude to the fisherman's story of the siren, the sight of whom converts his brother Giuseppe to a weeping wreck as he contemplates the inevitability of mortality. The legend declares that the child born of a pair who have seen the siren under water will save the world by destroying silence and marrying the siren. It is nearly fulfilled by Giuseppe and Maria;

but the priest intervenes, and Maria kills herself. The parents'
names are those of the parents of the infant Jesus; the clergy act
the part of Antichrist. Now the boatman is haunted by an
impossible dream; and it is that haunting, our being in the
presence of belief, our knowledge of the supernatural at second
hand, that lends power to the story. The madness induced by the
siren's face lingers on; but 'silence and loneliness cannot last
forever'. The dimension of true belief is the antithesis of spiritual
materialism, and survives persecution by the priests – and by the
tourists, for this story mentions an English lady who has written
a book which has turned the village into a showplace, and thus
corrupted it. The story of the siren is the story of the loss of vision
in the face of materialism and fear. It is an elusive tale, quite free
from allegory, but very moving in its evocation of a way of life
that is at once idealistic and robustly sane: there is nothing
charming or fey about the boatman. There is a strong sense of the
erotic, however, and the juxtaposition of the gleaming reality of
his brown body with the notes on the most impersonal of
religious controversies is a striking one. The demon boy here
becomes a beautiful and suffering man.

III

In all these tales of Pan we are aware less of a desire to entertain
than of a need to protest; and the stronger the protest the more
truly entertaining is the story. The power of Pan is believed in
not, as it were, metaphysically, as another mode of being, but
rather as a natural quality of life, to which these stories point
through the use of this particular literary convention. That
quality is the 'greater life among us', which Tommy wishes for
Harold in 'Albergo Empedocle'. It is not an escape into another
dimension, though under present conditions it has to be shown
as such. The flight of the lovers to the greenwood in *Maurice* is a
further example of this necessity.

　　In other tales Forster avoids the need to escape by writing
fables. There are five of these, and it is notable that they are
generally later in date than the Pan stories, and also that only
one, 'The Machine Stops', is set in the future. The others are
concerned with an after, or inner, life. 'The Machine Stops' does
indeed stand alone in the body of Forster's work, and is the most
impersonal of his tales. Yet it clearly stems from horror and

outrage at the transformations in human life which modern technology even then was bringing about. It contains much that was prophetic – the power of television, the reliance on experience at second hand, the architectural uniformity spread across the globe; and yet one can also read it as a critique of more immediate, comfortable suburban conditions by means of futuristic fantasy. The relationship between mother and son, in itself unusual in a story of this kind, gives it a far more intimate character than one might expect, though in this connection it is worth recalling Lionel Trilling's observation that the mothers in Forster's fiction 'have remarkably little impulse towards their sons'.[11] As always with Forster, generalised views are related to the personal life. In this tale too we have an element that is found in all his finest work – anger. Only through anger, controlled and disciplined, does he speak out.

But it is the absence of anger which is notable in the other fables. Two of them, 'Mr Andrews' and 'Co-ordination', are notably amiable in tone. Both are slight. In the former, the preference for friendship, rather than for friendship's reward in heaven, makes for one of Forster's softer tales, and the closing sentence almost amounts to self-parody: 'Then they suffered it to break in upon them, and they, and all the experience they had gained, and all the love and wisdom they had generated, passed into [the world soul], and made it better.' The tone here, as in 'Co-ordination' and 'The Celestial Omnibus', is comparable with that of Max Beerbohm in such tales as 'The·Small Boy and the Barley Sugar' or 'The Dreadful Dragon of Hay Hill'.[12] But the comparison is not in Forster's favour: he is too passionate to handle the sedate or mock-simple with assurance.

'Co-ordination', more truly light-hearted, is more successful, because the fantasy is less controlled, and full of Forster's own brand of mischief (his feeling for little girls is an example of this – Rose and Violet remind one of Minnie Beebe and Irma Herriton). This inconsequential little tale anticipates the portrayal of sublime cosmic muddle in *A Passage to India*. Both it and 'Mr Andrews' are pictures rather than stories; and George Thomson remarks with justice on 'how completely Forster's imagination deserted him when vision and anti-vision were expressed through the same characters or when the anti-vision was excluded'.[13]

'The Celestial Omnibus' is of sterner stuff, despite its playful opening. Mr Bons, like Leyland in 'The Story of a Panic', is a pseudo-aesthete, one who confuses books with their substance, the shadow with the reality; when transported to the world of books in its eternal state he cannot endure it, and falls to his death from the celestial omnibus, just as in other Forster stories books fall to the floor or into rivers. But the boy, the innocent eye, can flourish in the archetypal world which destroys the spiritual materialist. The tone of the story at times resembles Belloc's cheerfully sardonic *Bad Child's Book of Beasts* (1896) and is altogether less whimsical than other contemporary celebrations of childhood vision; but the method of the satire is all Forster's own, deft and telling in its dramatisations. Just as in 'The Story of the Siren' the narrator tells the boatmen that he has seen the siren 'often and often' (he is trying to be ironic), so here Mr Bons boasts of having seven Shelleys in his house. But the omnibus goes 'the whole way' and this is beyond his reach.

It is interesting to compare Forster's fantasy with a contemporary and much longer one which also deals with famous characters in fiction: Walter de la Mare's *Henry Brocken* (1904). This excessively bookish narrative is the kind of elusive dreaming which, if too highbrow for the boy's parents, would just suit Mr Bons. Forster is in fact assessing a literary tradition even while he is using it. (And his hero, significantly, is called The Boy.) A critique of literary historicism, anticipating that in *Aspects of the Novel,* occurs when Mr Bons asserts that the Duchess of Malfi was older than Mrs Gamp. The story may be in a whimsical tradition, but it uses the whimsy to make its points.

More truly original, however, is 'The Other Side of the Hedge'. This, an early tale, anticipates many of the themes of *The Longest Journey.* Miss Eliza, like Agnes later and memorably, rides a bicycle, and the distinction between those who see life as consisting of being on the move and those who see its essence as lying outside of time foreshadows the contrast between Herbert Pembroke and Stephen Wonham; it is significant that at the end it is a brother whom the narrator discovers. The allegorical element is strong, and the pool clearly represents a baptism. In its restrained, suggestive poetry, its impatient involvement with the world it denounces, 'The Other Side of the Hedge' is characteristic of Forster's sense of the unseen. As much as the later 'The Machine Stops', it constitutes an attack on the historicism of H. G. Wells.

Indeed, 'The Other Side of the Hedge' represents Forster's version of what may be called the 'great good place' theme, which Henry James had explored in his story of that name. In Forster's use of the term, however, there is not the sense of benevolent security which we find in James: indeed, 'The Machine Stops' might be read as his rejection of such an ideal. Instead he represents the place as being in the here and now, a dimension parallel, as it were, to our own, and known in that ecstatic communion which gives human life its highest value. This conception is indeed the 'point' of 'The Point of It', the story which, according to Forster, displeased his Bloomsbury friends. '"What *is* the point of it?" they queried thinly, nor did I know how to reply.' That 'thinly' places Forster's attitude to the Bloomsbury point of view rather well: the kind of self-regarding cultivation of qualitative response which they embodied was always the object of his satiric scrutiny. Leyland, Bons, what are they but the Bloomsbury ethic translated into suburban terms? But the cult of the ecstatic moment remained of importance to Forster, and was to provide him with a touchstone in the novels, besides being the subject of the richest of his tales, 'The Eternal Moment'.

In 'The Point of It', the ecstatic moment is known by the athlete Harold (that name again – it was also at one time to have been given to Stephen Wonham) as he overtaxes his strength while rowing. This veneration of the athlete is an endearing feature of Forster's early work (it even qualifies his portrayal of the odious Gerald Dawes in *The Longest Journey*) and is one of the things that stops his sense of the 'eternal moment' from being merely pictorial or aesthetic. The subsequent career of Harold's friend Sir Michael, who writes essays like those of A. C. Benson, ('Their good taste, their lucid style, the tempered Christianity of their ethics') is saved from being a morality piece or one-sided sketch by the dialogue overheard on his deathbed, in which the heartless comments of the sons echo the reader's own reactions with discomfiting effect. The final part of the tale, chronicling Sir Michael's posthumous existence in a sandy Hell, the presentation of which looks forward to the visionary world of Samuel Beckett, is easily the most serious and impressive thing that Forster was to write in this vein. Hell is inaction, sloth, the refusal of response: the end of the tale returns us to the moment when Harold died in ecstasy and when Sir Michael dies a second time into, it is implied, eternal life. No wonder the Bloomsburys disliked the story: it has a theological complexity beyond their normal imaginings. Forster here provides one more gloss on the 'great good place' theme. And what *was* the point of it? Again one is directed to values outside of time, an optimism of the moment. Forster's indictment of Sir Michael compares interestingly with what he has to say of Rickie Elliot in *The Longest Journey*.

The timeless moment is to be subject to more enigmatic treatment in one of the most admired stories, 'The Road to Colonus'. It is a sardonic and ambiguous tale, an old man's version of 'The Story of a Panic'. But possession here means vision. Forster's account of the Greek shrine anticipates his response to what he was to find in India.

> Little votive offerings to the presiding Power were fastened on to the bark – tiny arms and legs and eyes in tin; grotesque models of the brain or the heart – all tokens of some recovery of strength or wisdom or love. There was no such thing as the solitude of nature, for the sorrows and joys of humanity had pressed even into the bosom of a tree. He spread out his arms and steadied himself against the soft charred wood, and then slowly leant back, till his body was resting on the trunk behind. His eyes closed, and he had the strange feeling of one who is moving, yet at peace – the feeling of the swimmer, who, after long struggling with chopping seas, finds that after all the tide will sweep him to his goal.   (I)

The transition is beautifully done. The soured and weary Mr Lucas abandons himself to his moment of revelation in a manner that symbolises life in death; his subsequent removal from the place where, momentarily, he would end his days is placed with precision in the final episode, where, older but still alive, querulous and senile, he is told how he would have been killed by an earthquake had he stopped. The irony here is double. Not only is Mr Lucas too wrapped up in a letter to his landlord to take notice of his escape, but also the very things of which he is complaining in his letter are, as John Beer has pointed out, clearly subconscious memories of the life and surroundings that would have been his had he remained.[14] As it is, two modes of death are juxtaposed with an economy that is most effective. The point is presented to the reader, not thrust at him; nor is there any Edwardian whimsy in the references to the gods. The tale eschews the merely literary.

The literary is frequently the enemy where Forster is concerned: it is as though he had an inbuilt mistrust of his own methods. Nowhere is this more apparent than in 'The Eternal Moment'; but in 'Ansell' too, his earliest story of all, we see it no less clearly. Here we find him consigning a trunk-load of books into a mountain stream, and an entire scholar's career is weighed in the balance with the life known and lived by the coachman Ansell, the boyhood friend who is to reappear under his own name at Cambridge in *The Longest Journey* and anonymously as the gardener's boy in *Maurice*. The tale is so free from didacticism as to be almost too elusive; but this is a story the point of which it is *not* to have a point. What it presents is an attitude, an antithesis: the life of time, of careers, of scholarship, of prudence, set against the life of timelessness, the eternal moment extended into a knowledge of simple being. It is a marvellously accomplished tale for a beginner, and one that is singularly free from Edwardian influences. Not least of its jokes is the rescue of *Elizabeth and Her German Garden* from the river, for that book exemplifies much that Forster was to debunk. (The joke is improved when we remember that the story was written before Forster went to work for the authoress at Nassenheide.)

But the richest of all the tales is 'The Eternal Moment'; it is almost a miniature novel. Miss Raby is that most dangerous figure in Forster's world, the 'mildly unconventional person'. She declines the kind of marriage that Lilia Herriton makes in *Where Angels Fear to Tread*, meanly distrusting the young guide who professes love for her. 'He was too cheap: he gave us more than our money's worth. That, as you know, is an ominous sign in a low-born person.' (I). At a stroke Forster strips bare the financial basis for the muddle in spiritual materialism. But Miss Raby is a sentimentalist as well: she cherishes a romantic dream based on her escapade, and turns it into a book which popularises the little resort she now comes back to visit, in company with a middle-aged admirer called, once again, Leyland. If in outlook she resembles Helen Schlegel, in appearance she suggests, with her 'kind angular face', Adela Quested or Margaret Schlegel – those plain women who are, in Forster's world, the most sensitive recorders. Miss Raby, like them, is forced to see the conse-

quences of her own shortsightedness, in this case the vulgarisation of Vorta consequent upon the success of her novel. She has
exploited her own failure of moral vision, and the result is a moral
landslide, itself symbolised by the physical landslide which
destroys Signora Cantu's little farm.

> A landslip, in that valley, never hurried. Under the green coat
> of turf water would collect, just as an abscess is formed under
> the skin. There would be a lump on the sloping meadow, then
> the lump would break and discharge a slowly-moving stream
> of mud and stones. Then the whole area seemed to be cor
> rupted; on every side the grass cracked and doubled into
> fantastic creases, the trees grew awry, the barns and cottages
> collapsed, all the beauty turned gradually to indistinguishable
> pulp, which slid downwards till it was washed away by some
> stream.   (II)

The tangible excellence of the writing induces confidence in what
the author is telling us: the portrayal of the fortunes of Vorta is
precise and delicate. Significantly, the landslide also threatens
the bell tower, which is both the symbol of Miss Raby's achievement and the celebration of her defeat. But Forster's account of
that defeat is more convincing than the celebration of her victory.

> Her life had been successful, and on the whole happy. She was
> unaccustomed to that mood, which is termed depressed, but
> which certainly gives visions of wider, if greyer, horizons.
> That morning her outlook altered. She walked through the
> village, scarcely noticing the mountains by which it was still
> surrounded, or the unaltered radiance of its sun. But she was
> fully conscious of something new: of the indefinable corrup
> tion which is produced by the passage of a large number of
> people.

The scene in which Miss Raby confronts Feo and attempts to
discuss their past relationship is desolating: Feo has indeed been
corrupted into just that mercenary servant she had suspected
him of being. The conclusion is masterly in its irony; for we are
all but compelled to endorse the worldly-wise cheap cynicism of
Colonel Leyland, as the two men put their heads together against
the female threat. (But then the world of Goneril and Regan is

always plausible.)

IV

Forster's short stories are in many ways the key to his novels: certainly they direct our attention to what is singular about them. Although from its inception the English novel had been a vehicle for social and moral criticism, it did not, until the emergence of D. H. Lawrence, reflect a sense of personal alienation in its practitioners. Fielding, Jane Austen, Thackeray, even Dickens and George Eliot, had recognised and accepted the underlying social and economic structure: their criticisms (though this is only partly true of Dickens) took place in the region of personal, individual relationships. Hardy was perhaps the first novelist really to perceive the fundamental contradiction between what that society morally required and the means by which it maintained itself in being – which is why *Jude the Obscure* (1894) has some claim to be regarded as the first modern novel.

Forster's own personal and necessary alienation has already been referred to: it gave him a stance from which, as a novelist, he could survey the society of which he was such an uneasy part, and gauge his place in it. In the stories this process is seen in terms of deliverance, conversion, salvation – either proffered, accepted or denied. For him there is no fullness of life *within* society, and the whole relation of the novel to its setting and to its readers has become uneasy; as Raymond Williams observes, 'we can see these radical impulses straining almost dislocating his early novels'.[15] But Forster's art, the musicality of his deployment of narrative, commentary and symbol, safeguards him from the kind of warring vision which we find in a minor contemporary such as Machen. He remains part of his society in confining individual experience to a heightened consciousness and moral sense, in this differing radically from Lawrence. His art may look forward, but his outlook was derived from that nineteenth-century individualism so variously embodied in the writings of Matthew Arnold, George Eliot, and Walter Pater. 'The last Englishman' – in this particular sense Lawrence was right. But to be last is not necessarily to be left behind. The novels, even more than the stories, subject their premises to critical scrutiny. Forster, no less than Lawrence, was a writer in dialogue with himself, and thus among the earliest of the moderns.

5 Where Angels Fear to Tread

In his chapter 'The Plot' in *Aspects of the Novel*, Forster quotes an old lady with a healthy contempt for logic: 'How can I tell what I think till I see what I say?' It might be Mrs Honeychurch speaking. Elderly ladies are as plentiful in his fiction as they were in his life – Mrs Herriton, Mrs Failing, the two Miss Alans, Mrs Munt, Mrs Moore, to name a few (one notes that as each novel is published so their characters improve). It is certainly appropriate that another one should provide what might pass for their creator's fictional motto. It was through his imagination as much as through his personality or convictions that Forster learned to speak out. He used the domestic background which threatened him as a man to establish himself as an artist.

The people he writes about are middle-class, the class to which he himself belonged; and, except in the Cambridge chapters of *The Longest Journey* and in those describing the Schlegel sisters and their circle, he does not describe the kind of intellectual world to which he spiritually belonged and in which he felt at ease: it was home, Tunbridge Wells or Weybridge, the life with Mother, that he portrayed, with a rebellious spirit that was yet so aware of that life, so understanding of it, as almost to be disarmed by it. Forster has been castigated for not breaking free from maternal bonds; but at the deep level of artistic conscience he may have known that he was right to stay within them. Certainly his doing so lends cogency to his analysis of the world he called 'Sawston', even though it robs his work of the glamour of more overt rejections.

Forster lived for so long that it is easy to forget that he was an Edwardian whose first four novels appeared while Edward VII was still on the throne. But *Where Angels Fear to Tread* came out in the year following *The Golden Bowl*, *The Longest Journey* in the same year as *The Secret Agent*. *A Room with a View* is contemporary with *The Old Wives' Tale*, and *Howards End* with *The History Of Mr Polly*. All four novels antedate not only *Sons and Lovers*, *The Voyage Out* and *A Portrait of the Artist as a Young Man*, but also *Zuleika Dobson*, *The Unbearable Bassington*, *South Wind* and *Valmouth*. And it is against these last novels that we should measure those of E. M. Forster if we are to understand his modernity. If he was not a poor man's Henry James, neither was he just a rich man's Saki.

To bring those two names together, however, is to suggest where the particular quality of these early novels lies. That they have a Jamesian seriousness is indisputable – passage after passage demonstrates a concern with that inward integrity, that insistence on what makes for the springs of livingness, together with a feeling for social nuance, that are to be found in James's work. In both cases these qualities are found in a man naturally reserved, cautious and watchful, and dominated by parental pressures (both had formidable mothers). But the Jamesian subtleties are in Forster combined with a playful wit, a bitterness and even a lurking savagery that suggests the author of *The Unbearable Bassington*. Forster was only twenty-six years old when *Where Angels Fear to Tread* was published: these are the novels of an Edwardian young man.

The youthfulness produces the uncertainty, the jumps; it is vitality which appears to outrage the canons of the Edwardian literary scene. (Indeed, only one of Forster's tales seems to belong in tone and subject matter with the more formal products of the period: this is 'The Helping Hand' – an ironic story, about an over-helpful wife, that was first published in *The Life to Come*. It seems especially tailored for the magazines, the kind of story that Agnes in *The Longest Journey* wanted Rickie to try his hand at. By a nice irony it describes an officiousness the equal of her own.) When we compare a Forster novel with one that is more characteristic of the period, say Galsworthy's *The Man of Property* (1906), we are immediately aware of the apparent lack of deliberation in the former, and of a feeling of organic growth, even of the exploratory inconsequence of the old lady quoted earlier. It is true that in *The Longest Journey* there is a show of structuring through threefold division (Cambridge, Sawston, Wiltshire) such as we find in contemporary authors such as Arnold Bennett or Hugh Walpole; but the other novels show few signs of knowing where they are bound for. 'How can I tell what

I think till I see what I say?' Either Forster didn't know, or his is the art that conceals art. In either case, for all his contempt for the story as an art form, he certainly knew how to tell one. The narrative momentum of the novels is irresistible.

This is especially true of *Where Angels Fear to Tread*. It exemplifies at the very start his preoccupations as a novelist; and it is accordingly the best one of his novels for a newcomer to read first. This is the story Forster tells:

Lilia Herriton, a slapdash young widow and a social embarrassment to her husband's family, is shipped off by them for a holiday in Italy, chaperoned by Caroline Abbott, a staid local girl ten years younger than herself. While visiting the small hill town of Monteriano (Forster based his descriptions on San Gimignano) she falls in love with Gino Carella, the son of a dentist, and becomes engaged to him. Her brother-in-law, Philip Herriton, is dispatched by his mother to investigate matters (a situation reminiscent of Henry James's *The Ambassadors*, published two years earlier); but on his arrival he finds Lilia already married. After a disillusioning time as a wife, she dies in childbirth. The Herritons ignore the baby until his father starts to send postcards to Irma, Lilia's daughter by her first marriage, a little girl whom they are bringing up. Caroline Abbott offers to adopt the baby, which is enough for Mrs Herriton to send out a second embassy, this time consisting of Philip and his bossy sister Harriet, in order to persuade Gino to give up his child to them. Caroline travels there independently in the hope of preventing this. Gino refuses to surrender his son; Philip and Caroline succumb once more to the charms of Italy, and do nothing; while Harriet goes straight ahead and kidnaps the child. But there is an accident (appropriately enough a collision of the Herriton's carriage with Caroline's) and the baby dies. Philip, having been half-killed by the enraged Gino, is left with a dawning love for Caroline, only to find that she is herself hopelessly in love with Gino. The invasion of Italy by the English ends in total defeat for them all.

This grim conclusion is not presaged in the novel's opening: 'They were all at Charing Cross to see Lilia off – Philip, Harriet, Irma, Mrs Herriton herself.' The words hold a note of desperation: anything to get the novel started, one feels. The fact was that Forster already had behind him two attempts at what was to end up as *A Room with a View*, false starts that failed to get anything really said. *Where Angels Fear to Tread* begins with a plunge, and the momentum of the opening is never really lost.

As an opening, however casually or deliberately arrived at, it has an immediacy rarely encountered in English fiction up till then, and seems almost insolently casual. But part of Forster's skill as a novelist is to produce such an impression of carelessness: we are won by the very modesty of the means employed to interest us. Something so unstudied *must* be true. But the opening of the novel is more clever than might at first appear. If we are to compare it with any other one, it would have to be with the enthralling first sentence of *Jane Eyre:* 'There was no possibility of taking a walk that day.' In those ten words Charlotte Brontë puts us into the position of overhearing her tale: 'that' day – it is assumed that we know which one it was. No wonder Smith Elder's reader was impressed.

Forster's technique is to assume that the reader knows whom he is talking about: the insertion of 'herself' after Mrs Herriton shows that. The tone is confidential. He is talking to a readership of equals in a way which no other novelist since Jane Austen had succeeded in doing. Indeed, this is one of Forster's finest gifts as a novelist: no one is more economical in method. As John Colmer says, 'By means of a deft social shorthand, he evokes the Edwardian world with all its minute particularities and social shibboleths, thus avoiding the laboured documentation of the Edwardian realists, Galsworthy, Bennett, and Wells.'[1] This is fiction being written out of a shared world, not primarily to entertain, nor to impress or argue: simply a 'thus it was, and is', and a confident appeal to us to share the implications of what is being said.

Those implications are clear from the first page onward. The antithesis between England and Italy is established at once in Philip's parting injunction to the feckless Lilia: 'See the little towns. . . . And don't, let me beg you, go with that awful tourist idea that Italy's only a museum of antiquities and art. Love and understand the Italians, for the people are more marvellous than the land' (Ch. 1). Even from the little we already know of Lilia ('ungovernable laughter', 'sprawling out of her first-class carriage') we can see that this is a priggish, unreal speech; at the same time we are aware that the sentiments are commendable. But that 'let me beg you' is tell-tale for a farewell message at the station. Philip is someone who does not know how to talk to people.

The kind of love for Italy that this speech betrays, the sense of Italy as a liberating force on Anglo-Saxon temperaments, is a personalising, almost domesticating, of the more romantic approach associated in the previous century with the poems of Robert Browning. It was, in Forster's wake, to have a number of successors. Norman Douglas's *South Wind* (1917), Huxley's *Those Barren Leaves* (1923) and Elizabeth Bowen's *The Hotel* (1927) play interesting variations on the theme – as does Noël Coward's song 'At the Bar on the Piccolo Marina', in this case with a spry frivolity that definitively parodies the whole tradition. But go back to the pioneering novel, and we find a very different and sobering picture. The distinction between Italy and England (or, rather, Sawston, Forster's emblematic suburban town) is the distinction between a mess and a muddle, one that is to be worked through again in *A Passage to India*.

Sawston exists in this novel merely as a state of mind. Caroline defines it perfectly.

> I hated the idleness, the stupidity, the respectability, the petty unselfishness. . . . I had got an idea that every one here spent their lives in making little sacrifices for objects they didn't care for, to please people they didn't love; that they never learnt to be sincere – and, what's as bad, never learnt how to enjoy themselves. (Ch. 5)

In his first three books Forster is engaged in a running battle with this world. Its definition may seem parochial; but as he was to demonstrate here (and conclusively in his last novel) tragedy can happen as a result of it. A whole civilisation, almost, is in the balance with Caroline's question to Philip, 'Do you want the child to stop with his father, who loves him and will bring him up badly, or do you want him to come to Sawston, where no one loves him, but where he will be brought up well?' Because of muddle, the child does neither.

Italy, unlike Sawston, is a physical presence rather than a state of mind; or, rather, it begins essentially as a state of mind for Philip, but then proceeds to assert its vital, and vitalising, otherness. Philip, like Mr Bons, is a pseudo-aesthete. He is intelligent enough to learn, but it is by his physical responses that he is saved. Forster's Italy is real. Compare this church with what Harriet's St James would have been like – pitch-pine pews, encaustic tiles, polished brass, and Sung Mattins at eleven:

> There had been a festa two days before, and the church still smelt of incense and of garlic. The little son of the sacristan was sweeping the nave, more for amusement than for cleanliness, sending great clouds of dust over the frescoes and the scattered worshippers. The sacristan himself had propped a ladder in the centre of the Deluge – which fills one of the nave spandrels – and was freeing a column from its wealth of scarlet calico. Much scarlet calico also lay upon the floor – for the church can look as fine as any theatre – and the sacristan's little daughter was trying to fold it up. She was wearing a tinsel crown. The crown really belonged to St Augustine. But it had been cut too big: it fell down over his cheeks like a collar – you never saw anything so absurd. One of the canons had unhooked it just before the festa began, and had given it to the sacristan's daughter.   (Ch. 8)

This resembles Samuel Butler's rather less affectionate mockery in *Alps and Sanctuaries* (1882) and elsewhere; but, more importantly, it anticipates the great celebration of cosmic mess in the third part of *A Passage to India*. What is immediately apparent is the love which informs the writing; and the artful note about the spandrel, and the sudden colloquialism of 'you never saw anything so absurd'. The effect of the latter is delicately to avoid any sense of patronage in the description, since the expression itself is Sawston language, and thus the judgement in this context recoils upon itself. It is, in a different tone, what Harriet might have said.

Forster's account of the legend of St Deodata contrasts in an interesting manner with Norman Douglas's picture of St Dodekanus, which was published twelve years later. Here is Douglas:

> He was born in A.D. 450, or thereabouts, in the city of Kallisto in Crete. He was an only child, a beautiful but unruly boy, the despair of his widowed mother. At the age of thirteen he encountered, one evening, an elderly man of thoughtful mien, who addressed him in familiar language. On several later occasions he discoursed with the same personage, in a

grove of laurels and pines known as Alephane; but what passed between them, and whether it was some divine apparition, or merely a man of flesh and blood, was never discovered, for he seems to have kept his mother in ignorance of the whole affair. From that time onward his conduct changed. He grew pensive, mild, and charitable. He entered, as youthful acolyte, a neighbouring convent of Salacian monks, and quickly distinguished himself for piety and the gift of miracles. In the short space of three years, or thereabouts, he had healed eight lepers, caused the clouds to rain, walked dryshod over several rivers, and raised twenty-three persons from the dead.[2]

Now for Forster on St Deodata:

She was a holy maiden of the Dark Ages, the city's patron saint, and sweetness and barbarity mingle strangely in her story. So holy was she that all her life she lay upon her back in the house of her mother, refusing to eat, refusing to play, refusing to work. The devil, envious of such sanctity, tempted her in various ways. He dangled grapes above her, he showed her fascinating toys, he pushed soft pillows beneath her aching head. When all proved vain he tripped up the mother and flung her downstairs before her very eyes. But so holy was the saint that she never picked her mother up, but lay upon her back through all, and thus assured her throne in Paradise. She was only fifteen when she died, which shows how much is within the reach of any schoolgirl. (Ch. 6)

Douglas's irony and faint lubricity seem rather heavy after this: he writes as though out of the pious tradition, undermining it from within: our attention is fixed more on the authorial performance than on the nature of the beliefs portrayed. Forster, on the other hand, while more open in his mockery, is really more reverential, for there is a high-spirited delight in the absurdities which makes for love. Douglas is more inclined to sneer. (Nevertheless, it is only fair to point out that, if we are to look for a brief statement of what Italy means in contrast to the world of Sawston, we shall find it in *South Wind*: 'Vices. My dear bishop! Under a sky like this. Have a good look at it; do.')

Forster's satire helps to maintain a moral balance. The rejection of Sawston does not involve a total acceptance of its opposite; or, rather, Forster sees that the alternative is not an absolute, for Italy, too, has its codes, as Lilia is soon to realise.

> Italy is such a delightful place to live in if you happen to be a man. There one may enjoy that exquisite luxury of Socialism – that true Socialism which is based not on equality of income or character, but on the equality of manners. In the democracy of the *caffè* or the street the great question of our life has been solved, and the brotherhood of man is a reality. But it is accomplished at the expense of the sisterhood of women. (Ch. 3)

It is a mark of Forster's comprehensiveness that he should make this point. (Significantly, his portrait of the Schlegel sisters in *Howards End* is far more real and less sentimental than are his pictures of male comradeship – perhaps because he was not embarrassed with sexual self-consciousness where female relationships were concerned.)

If Italy is a masculine world, in Sawston the women dominate. And in a masculine world Philip is at a loss: he is no match for Gino. Gino is Forster's most interesting incarnation of the demon boy. With his spontaneity, his mercurialism and successful masculinity he is everything that Philip is not, and is potentially the ideal brother who can bring fulfilment. But he is also conventional, covetous and violent. His twisting of Philip's broken arm may be symbolically appropriate; but it is in character, and indicates the dangerous side of the Pan element that lurks in Gino. Until *A Passage to India* it is almost the only appearance of savagery in Forster's work.

Not that violence is absent in Sawston: it is merely more controlled. The essential heartlessness, the Goneril-and-Regan aspect of its way of life, is well caught in Philip's conversation with his mother following Lilia's departure.

> 'Here beginneth the New Life,' said Philip.
> 'Poor child, how vulgar!' murmured Mrs Herriton. 'It's surprising that she isn't worse. . . .'
> 'I pity Miss Abbott. Fortunately one admirer is chained to England. Mr Kingcroft cannot leave the crops or the climate or something. I don't think, either, he improved his chances

today. He, as well as Lilia, has the knack of being absurd in public.'

Mrs Herriton replied, 'When a man is neither well-bred, nor well-connected, nor handsome, nor clever, nor rich, even Lilia may discard him in time.'

'No. I believe she would take anyone. Right up to the last, when her boxes were packed, she was "playing" the chinless curate. Both the curates are chinless, but hers had the dampest hands. I came on them in the Park. They were speaking of the Pentateuch.' (Ch. 1)

Here the brittle tone is characteristically Edwardian (the last two sentences might be out of a tale by Saki) and was to be carried over into the sophisticated drawingroom comedies of the 1920s and 1930s, in what may be called the Noël Coward manner. This feminine world has a ruthlessness normally associated with the male. When Mrs Herriton discovers that Caroline is preparing to adopt Lilia's child, she returns to the house 'in the most extraordinary condition' of rage, which startles Philip. 'This outburst of violence from his elegant ladylike mother pained him dreadfully. He had not known that it was in her.' But the reader knows. There is a telling moment after Philip's dispatch on the first abortive rescue operation. Mrs Herriton had been sowing peas, and while doing so received the news of Lilia's engagement.

> Just as she was going upstairs she remembered that she never covered up those peas. It upset her more than anything, and again and again she struck the banisters with vexation. Late as it was, she got a lantern from the toolshed and went down the garden to rake the earth over them. The sparrows had taken every one. But countless fragments of the letter remained, disfiguring the tidy ground. (Ch. 1)

The symbolism is typical of Forster; but so also is his refusal to filter the novel through any single point of consciousness. He remains in charge, the novelist who is telling us the story. And through these means, through our knowing of Mrs Herriton's violence before Philip does, we can keep on seeing the latter with the necessary detachment. The episode of the peas is a small one; but it is a sign of the instinctive novelist that Forster should make his points this way.

In Philip's sister Harriet the violence erupts: it is she, rather than Philip, who is like the conventional male. She is also the nearest thing we find in Forster's fiction to a comic butt; but even so he treats that role in his own way.

> [Mrs Herriton] saw her at last, two turnings away, vainly trying to shake off Mr Abbott, Miss Caroline Abbott's father. Harriet was always unfortunate. At last she returned, hot, agitated, crackling with bank-notes, and Irma bounced to greet her, and trod heavily on her corn. (Ch. 1)

This is excellent broad humour of its kind; but it is that 'Harriet was always unfortunate' which supplies the Forsterian touch: it puts the reader inside the family world, and, momentarily, on Mrs Herriton's side. Phrases such as this help to create the peculiarly intimate flavour of Forster's early novels.

Harriet's role is more complex than at first appears. She is the one who acts, however disastrously; and within the narrow limits of her imagination she is strictly honest – always a virtue in Forster's eyes. And the very high spirits with which he writes of her offsets any young-man sourness the novel might otherwise possess. It is certainly a young man's exuberance which goes to the account of the brother and sister's journey across Italy, an example of the author's comic writing at its best.

> And on the second day the heat struck them, like a hand laid over the mouth, just as they were walking to see the tomb of Juliet. From that moment everything went wrong. They fled from Verona. Harriet's sketch-book was stolen, and the bottle of ammonia in her trunk burst over her prayer book, so that purple patches appeared on all her clothes. Then, as she was going through Mantua at four in the morning, Philip made her look out of the window because it was Virgil's birthplace, and a smut flew in her eye, and Harriet with a smut in her eye was notorious. At Bologna they stopped twenty-four hours to rest. It was a festa, and children blew bladder whistles night and day. 'What a religion!' said Harriet. The hotel smelt, two puppies were asleep in her bed, and her bedroom window looked into a belfry, which saluted her slumbering form every quarter of an hour. Philip left his walking-stick, his socks, and the Baedeker at Bologna; she only left her sponge-bag. Next

day they crossed the Apennines with a train-sick child and a hot lady, who told them that never, never before had she sweated so profusely. 'Foreigners are a filthy nation,' said Harriet. 'I don't care if there are tunnels; open the windows.' He obeyed, and she got another smut in her eye. Nor did Florence improve matters. Eating, walking, even a cross word would bathe them both in boiling water. Philip, who was slighter of build, and less conscientious, suffered less. But Harriet had never been to Florence, and between the hours of eight and eleven she crawled like a wounded creature through the streets, and swooned before various masterpieces of art. It was an irritable couple who took tickets to Monteriano.   (Ch. 6)

This is more than an amusing chapter of accidents: the whole passage illuminates the characters of Harriet (the ammonia, the prayer book, her comments, her automatic tourism), of Philip (Virgil's birthplace, 'he obeyed') and of Italy itself (the festa, the belfry, the hot lady), the interaction of which makes for the immediate comedy, and the characteristics of which form the more remote comedy of the book as a whole. And the pacing of events, the typically intimate touch of 'Harriet with a smut in her eye was notorious' and the dependence on fact rather than embroidered fact (there is only one simile in the entire passage, and that an effective one) – all these things make for comic writing of a high order. But to analyse further would be heavy-handed: the points are obvious.

The farce, however, soon turns black. Harriet, brave, true to her lights, precipitates the crisis and brings about the baby's death: her acrid, indissoluble character is that of a killer. Yet Forster preserves her identity: she is acted upon by her upbringing. And, if we laugh at her, it is as Mrs Herriton and Philip laugh. The mirth recoils upon the reader.

But it is Philip and Caroline who are the centre of the book: between them there runs a continuous dialogue – indeed, they constitute an internal dialogue that is the novel's heart. Philip's ideals are to be ironically fulfilled for him as Lilia's are for her. At the very beginning we see him 'choking in the fog', and his pride in being unconventional only puts him in his mother's power. Mrs Herriton's rule is, 'Let Philip say what he likes, and he will let us do what we like.' The visit to Italy after Lilia's engagement is his first chance to prove himself. 'It was the first time he had had anything to do.' One seems to hear the author's own voice here; and certainly his portrait is a friendly one. 'The world, he found, made a niche for him as it did for every one. Decision of character might come later – or he might have it without knowing. At all events he had got a sense of beauty and a sense of humour.' The clash between Philip's aesthetic sense and the terms of his daily life produce disillusionment: 'He concluded that nothing could happen, not knowing that human love and love of truth sometimes conquer where love of beauty fails.' Forster then proceeds to develop the English veneration of a sense of humour: 'If he could not reform the world, he could at all events laugh at it, thus attaining at least an intellectual superiority.' (Ch. 5).

What Philip embodies is that self-protective irony which is the middle-class Englishman's defence against reality. Forster was one of the first people to analyse and portray it. Philip's attitude before the second expedition guarantees its failure in more ways than one.

> Philip saw no prospect of good, nor of beauty either. But the expedition promised to be highly comic. He was not averse to it any longer; he was simply indifferent to all in it except the humours. . . . There was nothing to distract him this time; his sentimentality had died, so had his anxiety for the family honour. He might be a puppet's puppet, but he knew exactly the disposition of the strings. (Ch. 6)

Philip has disowned all responsibility, and as a result, when the vital decision has to be taken concerning the child's future, he is paralysed. He is damned finally by Caroline's would-be friendly verdict: 'I dare tell you this because I like you – and because you're without passion; you look on life as a spectacle; you don't enter it; you only find it funny or beautiful' (Ch. 10).

Indeed, it is Caroline, rather than Philip, who provides the living centre of the book, even though we are never taken inside her mind. Forster makes of her a foredoomed spinster, at twenty-two able to chaperon even the slipshod Lilia. She and Philip provide a duality in counterpoint. Initially she is on the defensive, as when she has to break the news of Gino's status to Philip, who at this moment is the very embodiment of Sawston respectability.

> 'Well, I don't suppose you'll think it a good match. But that's
> not the point. I mean the point is not – I mean that social
> differences – love, after all – not but what –'
> Philip ground his teeth together and said nothing.
> 'Gentlemen sometimes judge hardly. But I feel that you, and
> at all events your mother – so really good in every sense, so
> really unworldly – after all, love – marriages are made in
> heaven.'
> 'Yes, Miss Abbott, I know. But I am anxious to hear
> heaven's choice. You arouse my curiosity. Is my sister-in-law
> to marry an angel?'
> 'Mr Herriton, don't – please, Mr Herriton – a dentist. His
> father's a dentist.' (Ch. 2)

It is surprising nowadays to realise the social difference that
existed in England at that time between doctors and dentists;
however, Forster's skilful handling of the dialogue makes it
plausible. Indeed, his use of dialogue is always good: no novelist
has had a surer ear for the telling phrase or cadence, and
Elizabeth Bowen did well to call him 'the master dialogue-writer
of our century'.[3]

The first failure of Caroline and Philip in the face of Lilia's
marriage results in a joint collapse. When Gino playfully pushes
Philip onto a bed, the latter interprets it as an assault, thus with
unconscious irony prefiguring Gino's later, genuine attack;
Caroline weeps and begs him to take her away. The proprieties
have most ludicrously failed. But – significantly, under Mrs
Herriton's pressure – Caroline rebels, and refuses to be brow-
beaten, thus reacting in a way that Philip is powerless to do. It is
her resolve to adopt the child which sends Philip and Harriet to
Italy in her wake. Once there, both she and Philip respond to the
life they find in Monteriano, and most especially to the fact of
Gino's fatherhood: the place, Italy, brings about a momentary
unity. But Philip's renewed worry about the child dissolves it.

> All the pleasure and the light went out of her face, and she
> became again Miss Abbott of Sawston – good, oh, most
> undoubtedly good, but most appallingly dull. Dull and re-
> morseful: it is a deadly combination, and he strove against it in

vain. . . .   (Ch. 6)

At the final crisis Caroline rounds on him and there is a complete reversal of roles.

> Oh, what's the use of your fairmindedness if you never decide for yourself? Anyone gets hold of you and makes you do what they want. And you see through them and laugh at them – and do it. It's not enough to see clearly; I'm muddle-headed and stupid, and not worth a quarter of you, but I have tried to do what seemed right at the time. And you – your brain and your insight are splendid. But when you see what's right you're too idle to do it. You told me once that we shall be judged by our intentions, not by our accomplishments. I thought it a grand remark. But we must intend to accomplish – not sit intending on a chair.   (Ch. 8)

The book ends on that note, modified only by Philip's making of the whole experience some kind of 'eternal moment' for himself. The novel's bright, clear, sardonic surface covers an inward grief. The control is absolute (only *A Passage to India* is equally free from sentimental passages) but at a cost. There is no satisfying resolution. 'For all the wonderful things had happened.' Philip's pessimistic conclusion is not refuted. The final sentence however is enigmatic. 'They hurried back to the carriage to close the windows lest the smuts should get into Harriet's eyes.' If Philip's attitude is to be taken seriously, that line is a flippant evasion of a solemnity that has been found embarrassing; if it is to be qualified, then this is a delicate way out of an optimistic refutation. The ambiguity is very characteristic of Forster's art.

The book is easily the most watertight of the Edwardian novels. Its economy and speed are quite remarkable; detail is set before us in a manner that is almost cinematic, carefully placed, always there to serve an end, and yet seemingly informal, casual. It is a notable act of rebellion against the Late Victorian afflatus of sentiment and literary expression. Its message, so to call it, is perfectly embodied in its form.

For all the brilliance of its presentation, however, that message constitutes a muted beginning for a novelist's career. It diagnoses a disease, but hardly moves towards prescribing for a cure. The novel's tonic qualities are the result of the willingness to define the grounds of what is amiss, and the consequent suggestion that to some extent an honourable defeat can be regarded as a victory – a view, however, which Caroline rebuts forcibly. Certainly the honour of this particular defeat is shaky, and Philip and Caroline are both left with Miss Raby's dilemma on their hands. One is aware that the moment glimpsed and lost, the moment of revelation, for example, when they watch Gino with his child, can easily become an idol. The dangerous pleasures of self-martyrdom are frequently the consequence of a too-ready acceptance of defeat; and Sawston waits to reclaim her erring sons and daughters. In his next novel Forster was to examine further the problems of emotional frustration, and the perils of compensatory romanticism that accompany it. It was a gallant thing to do, but ironically itself resulted in an honourable defeat.

6 The Longest Journey

The Longest Journey was Forster's own favourite among his novels, because 'in it I have managed to get nearer than elsewhere towards . . . that junction of mind with heart where the creative impulse sparks'.[1] It is an interesting comment, not least because the success of the novel has always been called in question, and opinions about it have probably been more divided than in the case of any of the others except, possibly, *Howards End*. But this very fact bears out Forster's comment: *The Longest Journey* holds the key to his particular message and gifts as a creative artist. Dismiss it, and you are outside the pale where you can really understand the other novels. But accept it uncritically and you find yourself committed to a valuation that narrows the author's achievement to that of a novelist concerned merely with self-fulfilment. The extensions of a personal crisis into discussions of a general social situation, which give the other books their authority and poise, are equally present in this one; and in assessing it they must be taken into account when considering what is in many respects a characteristic second novel, an experiment of questionable success following on a more restricted but satisfying first venture. It is certainly a more personal book than its predecessor; and if we are to place the novels in pairs (there is a good case to be made for doing so) it stands with the posthumously published *Maurice*; the two books may most usefully be read in each other's light.

The story of *The Longest Journey* is even bleaker than that of *Where Angels Fear to Tread*. Rickie Elliot is the crippled son of a crippled father, an orphan and, when the novel opens, an undergraduate at Cambridge. An arch-romantic, he falls in love with the love affair between Agnes Pembroke and Gerald Dawes, despite his well-justified dislike of the latter. But Gerald is killed playing Rugby football, and in due course Rickie himself becomes engaged to Agnes, in the firm conviction that he is second best. On a visit to Wiltshire, to stay with his father's

74

sister Mrs Failing, he discovers that Stephen Wonham, an amiable scapegrace whom his aunt has brought up, is his half-brother. Assuming that Stephen is the child of his hated father, he agrees with Agnes to keep the matter secret, even from Stephen himself. After his marriage he settles down as assistant to Agnes's brother Herbert Pembroke, who is housemaster at Sawston, a minor public school, and passes increasingly under the Pembrokes' influence, despite the protests of his Cambridge friend, Stewart Ansell. But Mrs Failing tells Stephen the truth about his birth, and he comes to Sawston to claim kinship. The Pembrokes, thinking that he is attempting blackmail, try to buy him off; but Ansell, who knows the truth, reveals that Stephen is the son of Rickie's beloved mother. The shock of this disclosure results in Rickie's leaving his wife and devoting himself to Stephen, in hopes of reforming him. The attempt is terminated by his death, the result of pulling the drunken Stephen off a level crossing in the path of an oncoming train.

Even more than in *Where Angels Fear to Tread*, Forster is concerned to provide us with an anti-hero. Or is he? The matter is central to any discussion of this novel. Rickie was so called by his father because he was rickety. However much this may rebound on the odious Mr Elliot, final responsibility rests with the author: the strange thing about this strangest of all Forster's novels is the way in which Rickie is hounded to his doom by his creator. Read from one point of view, the book seems like an exercise in self-hatred. In the light of the author's own oppressed sexual nature the symbolism is both obvious and painful: Forster is describing himself as he feels that the world must see him. And it would seem that he is tempted to endorse the world's verdict. Rickie is not only lame but congenitally lame, unsure of himself and ineffectual; his final sacrifice is half-hearted and disillusioned, and his epitaph, pronounced by Mrs Failing, is on 'one who has failed in all he undertook; one of the thousands whose dust returns to the dust, accomplishing nothing in the interval' (Ch. 34). Over thirty years before Graham Greene portrayed the little whiskey priest in *The Power and the Glory*, Forster had challenged the usual concepts of success and failure – and without having a theological joker up his sleeve. *The Longest Journey* does in fact play a dangerous game, in bewildering the reader and potentially alienating his sympathies.

Where there were two spheres of interest in *Where Angels Fear to Tread,* here there are three. Sawston has now become Forster's old school, Tonbridge; and its frame of mind is seen motivating a system that is fatally muddled in its priorities.

> [Rickie] thought of Renan, who declares that on the Acropolis at Athens beauty and wisdom do exist, really exist, as external powers. He did not aspire to beauty or wisdom, but he prayed to be delivered from the shadow of unreality that had begun to darken the world. For it was as if some power had pronounced against him – as if, by some heedless action, he had offended an Olympian god. Like many another, he wondered whether the god might be appeased by work – hard uncongenial work. Perhaps he had not worked hard enough, or had enjoyed his work too much, and for that reason the shadow was falling.
>   '– And above all, a schoolmaster has wonderful opportunities of doing good; one mustn't forget that.'
>   To do good! For what other reason are we here? Let us give up our refined sensations, and our comforts and our art, if thereby we can make other people happier and better.   (Ch. 16)

As analysis this is much to the point; it perfectly expresses the homosexual's ambivalent attitude to the society that would condemn him. And the effectiveness of the passage is furthered by Forster's literary method, whereby he contrives through that 'declares' to make Renan's thought something the reader will surely know and share; and by the way in which he proceeds, after Agnes's remarks (for they are hers) to present Rickie's thoughts as an exclamation of the author's own, with a hint of irony thrown in. It is through such effects that Forster wins over his readers; or repels them. It is nothing if not a personal approach.

The dominant figure in the Sawston chapters is Herbert Pembroke. While making him a richly comic character, Forster is alive to his good points. The delicacy of handling is revealed when he shows Rickie the school, for while the fallacies in the system are mercilessly exposed, Mr Pembroke's own motives, such as they are, are not impugned. But the Pembrokes, like the Herritons, are spiritual materialists. On Herbert, Forster comments, 'he had but one test for things – success'. An instance of this is to be found in Agnes's handling of Rickie's stories. Herbert urges her to push them, for his interest is in markets. Agnes thinks she knows better:

> I am getting to learn my wonderful boy. We speak a great deal about his work. He has just finished a curious thing called 'Nemi' – about a Roman ship that is actually sunk in some lake. I cannot think how he describes the things, when he has never seen them. If, as I hope, he goes to Italy next year, he should turn out something really good. (Ch. 8)

We have already seen her annotation on Forster's own 'Other Kingdom': she is among those who approve of allegory because it allows them to turn imaginative vision back into the world they know.

But, if Sawston is the object of easy satire hardening into anger, the portrait of Cambridge is far more complex. Forster's own devotion to the place was lasting; and the account of it here has the peculiarly Forsterian 'shared' quality. The account of the arrival at the railway station is an example of this. On the other hand, the author's very enthusiasm coats some passages with a patina of sentimentality: comic bedmakers, horse-play on the lawn, and Rickie's likening of the elms to dryads – all these come too easily; our assent is not, in these matters, simply to be had for the asking. The Cambridge scenes lack the assurance, the rich pattern of detail to be found in, say, the Oxford chapters in Compton Mackenzie's *Sinister Street* (1913).

Central to the Cambridge theme in the novel is the character of Stewart Ansell. A self-confessed intellectual who finds life in the world of books (but who is fully aware that he does so), he embodies that disinterested love of truth which his creator found in Cambridge at its best. Detached from the main action and reluctant that Rickie should involve himself with marriage and 'the World', he expresses many of the ideals of Lowes Dickinson from an ethical standpoint similar to that of G. E. Moore. The 'undergraduate high priest' of Foster's 'local shrine',[2] he does indeed provide the moral touchstone of the book. But only the moral one. When he meets Stephen in the Pembrokes' garden, Stephen knocks him down in play; it is as though Forster is saying that morality, even the kind of morality of self-fulfilment that Ansell represents, will only go so far.

Ansell is something of a self-made man. His father is a draper; and there are some characteristic touches when Forster considers the class factor in his relationship with Rickie.

> 'Listen to your money!' said Rickie. 'I wish I could hear mine. I wish my money was alive.'
> 'I don't understand.'
> 'Mine's dead money. It's come to me through about six dead people – silently.'
> 'Getting a little smaller and a little more respectable each time, on account of the death-duties.'
> 'It needed to get respectable.'
> 'Why? Did your people, too, once keep a shop?'
> 'Oh, not as bad as that! They only swindled. About a hundred years ago an Elliot did something shady and founded the fortunes of our house.'
> 'I never knew anyone so relentless to his ancestors. You make up for your soapiness towards the living.'   (Ch. 3)

The exchange sheds light not only on Rickie and Ansell, but on class attitudes towards money at the time. It is a measure of Rickie's difference from the Pembrokes that they would never be able to appreciate the force of his point of view.

Ansell from the very outset is the guardian of objective truth. 'The cow is there.' It is still there, even if there is no one there to see it; and so he is hostile to Rickie's day-dreaming. But he is even more hostile to the Pembrokes, for he sees through their pretensions. This is counterpointed by the Pembrokes' awareness of social superiority: Agnes's snubbing of Ansell's sister in the Army and Navy Stores reminds us of Ansell's refusal of her offered greeting, which left her with an outstretched hand 'longer than is maidenly'. The balance struck between approval and condemnation of his 'honesty' is very sure. But Ansell is the delineator of the truth to Rickie. 'My personal objections to Miss Pembroke are as follows: – (1) She is not serious. (2) She is not truthful.' So long as he is uttering Forsterian truths he is admirable; but outside of that there is nothing for him to do. His arrival in Sawston is as contrived as Stephen's own, and he degenerates into being Rickie's conscience. Really, he should be Rickie's lover: there are enough parallels between their companionship and that of Maurice and Clive in *Maurice* to warrant the assertion. As it is, the paean to friendship has an uncomfortable effect: too many veiled homosexual stories have been told in this way, from the novels of Forrest Reid to the blandishments of the Reverend Bill McGrath in Angus Wilson's *Hemlock and After* (1953). Indeed, the Cambridge episodes have altogether too clubby a ring to be the repository of counter-Sawston values. Though *counter*-Sawston is strictly what they are – 'anti-Forsyte', to quote Lawrence's term. It is not so far from the dismayed 'Ladies!' when Agnes and Mrs Lewin walk in, to the dismissive 'the women' of Gerald and of Charles Wilcox.

> 'Damn these particular women.'
> 'They looked and spoke like ladies.'
> 'Exactly. Their diplomacy was ladylike. Their lies were ladylike. They've caught Elliot in a most ladylike way . . . for one moment we were natural, and during that moment Miss Pembroke told a lie, and made Rickie believe it was the truth.'
> 'What did she say?'
> 'She said "we see" instead of "I see" . . . and she made him believe it was the truth. She caught him and makes him believe that he caught her. She came to see me and makes him think that it is his idea. That is what I mean when I say that she is a lady.' (Ch. 8)

The ladies in this instance are given a good innings. The initial impression of Agnes is not unfavourable, and her pride in her unconventionality, if mistaken, is rather touching: it is significant that the earrings she had donned for Gerald are abandoned when she marries Rickie. And in the figure of Mrs Lewin Forster embodies a whole social system of chaperonage.

> She was a typical May-term chaperon, always pleasant, always hungry, and always tired. Year after year she came up to Cambridge in a tight silk dress, and year after year she nearly died of it. Her feet hurt, her limbs were cramped in a canoe, black spots danced before her eyes from eating too much mayonnaise. But still she came, if not as a mother as an aunt, if not as an aunt as a friend. Still she ascended the roof of King's, still she counted the balls of Clare, still she was on the point of grasping the organization of the May races. 'And who is your friend?' she asked. (Ch. 7)

There is a Jamesian ring to this; but the placing of her question at the end of the paragraph and not as the opening of a dialogue (which it is) is pure Forster: it makes it a part of the description. It is what she must be forever asking, and is all the funnier for that.

But 'ladies' in the context of Rickie's and Ansell's world are not so much women as the threat to the delicate threads of male friendship. For *The Longest Journey* relates specifically to Shelley's *Epipsychidion*. The poem not only provides the title but also is referred to a number of times, most notably in the scene in which Rickie climbs up to Cadbury Rings and finds he has a brother. It voices Shelley's distrust of marriage and of the effects it can have upon the relations between the sexes. Forster's own distrust is always apparent: there is not one happy or truly fulfilling marriage in the succeeding novels, if we except that of Lucy and George at the end of *A Room with a View*; and that is more wedding than marriage. The only other possible exception is, ironically, the one between Clive and Anne in *Maurice*. But in addition (or contrast) to this, *The Longest Journey* shows us the adequately provided-for Rickie and Agnes being faced with a postponement of their wedding for financial reasons, till Rickie, like Gerald before him, has been able 'to make his way'. Rickie's glorifying of Gerald and Agnes's passion is something, however, which the author appears to endorse. Yet Rickie's offer of money to Gerald, so that they may gratify it legally with more speed, reflects not only his naïvety, but also his fatal spirit of compromise. Gerald's objection, that it is unhealthy, while unjust has point.

Agnes, indeed, is treated unfairly by her creator. It is true that her early charm manifestly conceals a ruthless possessiveness and aggression, all the more deadly for its mask of common sense; but the tone of the passage which describes her loss of her child grates badly. 'She had got over the tragedy; she got over everything.' In the context of this particular novel, and beside the author's usual compassion and friendliness, the comment is seriously damaging to our belief in the rest of the book. To display excessive animus against a character is always a novelist's undoing.

Vital to any measured response is the scene between Rickie and Agnes in the dell. The dell itself might well have provided the occasion for some lush or, worse, whimsical 'nature writing';

but not here. The dell is local, it is particular, it is still there; and now the new western Cambridge by-pass occupies a cutting between it and Madingley. It had, at the time in which the book is set, its brief period of romance; but it occasions also yet another of Forster's wary refutations of aestheticism.

> '*Procul este, profani!*' exclaimed a delighted aesthete on being introduced to [the dell]. But this was never to be the attitude of Rickie. He did not love the vulgar herd, but he knew that his own vulgarity would be greater if he forbade it ingress, and that it was not by preciosity that he would attain to the intimate spirit of the dell. Indeed, if he had agreed with the aesthete, he would possibly not have introduced him. If the dell was to bear any inscription, he would have liked it to be 'This way to Heaven', painted on a sign-post by the high-road, and he did not realize till later years that the number of visitors would not thereby have sensibly increased. (Ch. 2)

'This way to Heaven' recalls 'The Celestial Omnibus'; but even with the aid of that story it is difficult not to find the ascription sentimental. Does Forster himself? It is characteristic of the uncertain tone of this novel that the dell is the setting for Agnes's securing of Rickie for herself: he is trapped by the siren in the place of his own dreaming. And yet by all the promptings of his physical nature he is right to follow her, and the account of their meeting there is tender, and rings true; Forster, however, is concerned here with more than the physical laws of nature. The dell is Rickie's spiritual sanctuary which Agnes has invaded (am I alone in always thinking of her as taller than he is?) and what may be right for others is wrong for him. Moreover, the actual love scene has a strongly maternal character.

> 'Did you take me for the Dryad?' she asked. She was sitting down with his head on her lap. He had laid it there for a moment before he went out to die, and she had not let him take it away.
>
> 'I prayed you might not be a woman,' he whispered.
>
> 'Darling, I am very much a woman. I do not vanish into groves and trees. I thought you would never come to me.' . . .
>
> He started, and cried passionately, 'Never forget that your greatest thing is over. I have forgotten: I am too weak. You

shall never forget. What I said to you then is greater than what I say to you now. What he gave you then is greater than anything you will get from me.'

She was frightened. Again she had the sense of something abnormal. Then she said, 'What is all this nonsense?' and folded him in her arms.   (Ch. 7)

She does well to be frightened: it is abnormal, and abnormality will always terrify a mind for which the normal is the only good there is. But even on those terms the account is distressing: something deeply wrong has got into the book. Agnes *is* a real woman, but reality of any kind will now be hostile to Rickie, for he has chosen to ignore reality. There is a troubling ambiguity here, not an enriching one. If Rickie is right, our rejection of him will be all the easier; if he is wrong, the author is shirking the demonstration that he is so.

Or delaying: the rest of the book may be read as that demonstration. For the dell, the womb-like enclosure, is not, finally, the natural image that lingers in our minds: it may lead to Heaven, but Heaven it is not. The spacious landscape of Wiltshire is what dominates the novel, a place of masculine companionship and ancient memories, the place where Rickie is first offered the gift of a brother. It calls out some of Forster's most characteristic descriptive prose.

The Rings were curious rather than impressive. Neither embankment was over twelve feet high, and the grass on them had not the exquisite green of Old Sarum, but was grey and wiry. But Nature (if she arranges anything) had arranged that from them, at all events, there should be a view. The whole system of the country lay spread before Rickie, and he gained an idea of it that he never got in his elaborate ride. He saw how all the water converges at Salisbury; how Salisbury lies in a shallow basin, just at the change of the soil. He saw to the north the Plain, and the stream of the Cad flowing down from it, with a tributary that broke out suddenly, as the chalk streams do: one village had clustered round the source and clothed itself with trees. He saw Old Sarum, and hints of the Avon valley, and the land above Stonehenge. And behind him he saw the great wood beginning unobtrusively, as if the down too needed shaving; and into it the road to London slipped, covering the bushes with white dust. Chalk made the dust white, chalk made the water clear, chalk made the clean rolling outlines of the land, and favoured the grass and the distant coronals of trees. Here is the heart of our island: the Chilterns, the North Downs, the South Downs radiate hence. The fibres of England unite in Wiltshire, and did we condescend to worship her, here we should erect our national shrine.   (Ch. 13)

Wiltshire was a favoured county with Richard Jefferies and W. H. Hudson (the latter's *A Shepherd's Life* appeared three years after *The Longest Journey*) but here too Forster strikes his own note. The conversational tone is directed to a different kind of readership from that of those two writers; a more self-conscious, self-distrustful audience is in view. The description is deliberately non-emotive, but observant of the details that go to make this a humanised landscape, such as place-names, the dusty roads (still not tarmacadamed), the siting of the towns and villages: it is a rationalised description. But along with this there is the uneasy invoking of a religious spirit, the subtle, (in context too subtle), irony of 'did we condescend to worship her', which has the slightly belittling effect that weakens much of Forster's writing in this mode. Rickie does indeed see differently on his ride with Stephen: he had noted then that

The green of the turnips, the gold of the harvest, and the brown of the newly turned clods, were each contrasted with morsels of grey down. But the general effect was pale, or rather silvery, for Wiltshire is not a county of heavy tints. Beneath these colours lurked the unconquerable chalk, and wherever the soil was poor it emerged. The grassy track, so gay with scabious and bed-straw, was snow-white at the bottom of its ruts.   (Ch. 12)

Here the naturalistic particularities have a genuine poetry that allows Forster to move to more august evocations without self-consciousness and without a clash of tone.

A dazzling amphitheatre gleamed in the flank of a distant hill, cut for some Olympian audience. And here and there, whatever the surface crop, the earth broke into little embankments, little ditches, little mounds: there had been no lack of drama to solace the gods.

The last remark is thrown in tersely, in keeping with the precise observation that has gone before. The conception is given its due dignity, without sentimentalising rhetoric or windy oracles. Indeed, in all Forster's writing of this kind we find a bareness that is refreshing after all the lush overwriting that afflicts so many rural writers who followed in Hardy's wake – Eden Phillpotts and Mary Webb provide obvious examples. It may be beset by playfulness of the wrong kind, but this is balanced by sharp observation ('coronals of trees', 'morsels of grey down') and a kind of historical analysis. It is this balance of elements which marks the central episode of *The Longest Journey*, Rickie's denial of his brother. Here the portentous setting of the ancient earthwork, and the symbolism of Rickie's movement further into the circle, is offset by the sharpness of observation, and by the peculiar blend of frivolity and ruthlessness in Mrs Failing. In this scene, read mythologically, the Knight of the Grail is brought to the castle of Carbonek and fails to ask the vital question: which parent gave me my brother? His rejection of his father spills over onto Stephen, aided by his own fastidiousness and his adhesion to the false world of the Pembrokes; while the proprietorial attachment to his mother, foreshadowed in the episode of the dell, leads to his exploitation by the managerial father-world of Sawston. (Later, Stephen, the mother's child, is to complain that Rickie cannot keep his wife in line.) But these considerations are left implicit. There is no clumsy signposting.

Mrs Failing herself is perhaps the most interesting person in the novel, for she embodies opposing viewpoints such as we find in Forster himself, the hard and the soft. The soft is evident in her attitudes to art and nature.

> Mrs Failing's attitude towards Nature was severely aesthetic – an attitude more sterile than the severely practical. She applied the test of beauty to shadow and odour and sound; they never filled her with reverence or excitement; she never knew them as a resistless trinity that may intoxicate the worshipper with joy. If she liked a ploughed field it was only as a spot of colour – not also as a hint of the endless strength of the earth.   (Ch. 11)

Again, before she goes down, deliberately late, to greet Rickie and Agnes on their arrival for their fateful visit to her 'perilous house' she 'glanced at the poems of Milton' before going to them 'with uplifted hands of apology and horror'. But she is disposed to see through Agnes's pretensions of unconventionality, and tells Stephen not to shave before dinner. It is impossible (for this reader at any rate) not to feel a certain liking for her.

Her reactions are often anti-philistine; but Forster, modifying Arnold's attitudes, always has something to say in favour of the Philistine. (Possibly his belonging to an outlawed freemasonry which inevitably transcended class divisions made him more tolerant.) He certainly distinguished between philistines and those innocent of formal culture, between, say, the Wilcox family in *Howards End* and the Ansells. Mrs Failing's aestheticism is shallow, and her attitudes are contrasted with those of her husband, a writer whose memorial remains she is editing and whose thought and character have affinities with those of William Morris. Mrs Failing's softness leads her to amuse herself with Stephen, her hardness to dismiss him when he gets out of hand. Her lack of heart is constantly in evidence, a selfishness that masks itself within an ironic mockery of the world. But her intelligence, so far as it goes, always makes her worth listening to. Like all heretics, she is a distorter of something that is true. Her final scene with Rickie when she tries to persuade him to return to Agnes is one of the most effective that its author wrote.

She stretched out her hand to him with real feeling. 'It is easier now than it will be later. Poor lady, she has written to me foolishly and often, but, on the whole, I side with her against you. She would grant you all that you fought for – all the people, all the theories. I have it, in her writing, that she will never interfere with your life again.'

'She cannot help interfering,' said Rickie, with his eyes on the black windows. 'She despises me. Besides, I do not love her.'

'I know, my dear. Nor she you. I am not being sentimental. I say once more, beware of the earth. We are conventional people, and conventions – if you will but see it – are majestic in their way, and will claim us in the end. We do not live for great passions or for great memories or for anything great.'

He threw up his head. 'We do.'   (Ch. 34)

That defiance is not unexpected, for Rickie already has her measure: as he says to Agnes on their first visit to Cadover, 'Don't you think there are two great things in life that we ought to aim at – truth and kindness? Let's have both if we can, but let's be sure of having one or the other. My aunt gives up both for the sake of being funny' (Ch. 13). Ultimately Mrs Failing is aptly named (too aptly), for she is heartless: her plausible words to Rickie in their final meal together constitute a temptation which it is his salvation to have rejected. She is plausible, and even, on occasion, dangerously attractive. But her epitaph on Rickie must not be confused with the author's own.

If Mrs Failing is a case of ambiguity of a positive kind, the character of Stephen is baffling. He is a blend of nature boy, *anima naturaliter Christiana* and buffoon: almost a fool of God. Once again we have a romantic conception subjected defensively to deromanticising treatment. The initial presentation of him has a certain clumsiness; then the incident with the shepherd, whose flock he guards, reveals his innate generosity. But there is confusion: it is Mrs Failing's self-indulgent treatment of him which has made him what he is. Forster is certainly at pains to escape the charge of sentimentalising him: the drunkenness (though it is at times sentimentally defended) makes him unaccommodating, and the scene with the soldier on the way to Salisbury is as tiresome for the reader as it is for Rickie. But at other times Stephen becomes more glowingly the ideal friend, the brother foreshadowed in 'The Other Side of the Hedge', and also in the characterisation of his father, the farmer who raises Mrs Elliot to new life only to be, in keeping with the remorseless urge of his creator's imagination, drowned. He, Robert, does indeed anticipate many characters in the novels of D. H. Lawrence ('As he talked, the earth became a living being – or rather a being with a living skin, – and manure no longer dirty stuff, but a symbol of regeneration and of the birth of life from life' – Ch. 29). His contacts with the Elliot family have a still more Lawrentian ring:

> He became diplomatic, and called at Mr Elliot's rooms to find things out. For if Mrs Elliot was happier than he could ever make her, he would withdraw, and love her in renunciation. But if he could make her happier, he would love her in fulfilment. Mr Elliot admitted him as a friend of his brother-

in-law's, and felt very broadminded as he did so. Robert, however, was a success. The youngish men there found him interesting, and liked to shock him with tales of naughty London and naughtier Paris. They spoke of 'experience' and 'sensations' and 'seeing life', and when a smile ploughed over his face, concluded that his prudery was vanquished. He saw that they were much less vicious than they supposed: one boy had obviously read his sensations in a book. But he could pardon vice. What he could not pardon was triviality, and he hoped that no decent woman would pardon it either. There grew up in him a cold, steady anger against these silly people who thought it advanced to be shocking, and who described, as something particularly choice and educational, things that he had understood and fought against for years.

Not only the content of this passage but also some of the cadences of its prose anticipate Lawrence. The next paragraph begins, 'She had suffered terribly'.

As the novel proceeds one might expect Stephen to grow in stature; but, characteristically, although this does in the end happen, it does not happen smoothly. His quest for Rickie at Sawston reveals him at his most honourable (though the occasion for his visit is a blatant plot device); while the fact that he knocks Ansell down is some kind of 'placing'. It links him with the (again ambiguous) figure of Gerald Dawes, who could knock anyone down 'if he liked'. Forster's attitude to violence here is almost wistful: Stephen 'was in better spirits, as a man ought to be who has knocked down a man'. The verbal order is significant: it is knocking down a *man*, not the knocking down as such, which matters.

Forster refuses the simplicity of the conventional novel's ending. The relationship between the brothers, following what can almost be described as their elopement, is uneasy, and, for Rickie disillusioning. He can only partly realise that Stephen has rescued him in the same way that Robert had rescued their mother. Nor is their relationship especially happy for the reader: Forster has a tiresome habit of making young men romp. But the final chapter, which shows Stephen married (and how skilfully Forster contrives to suggest a happy marriage without at the same time challenging comparison with Rickie's unhappy one) is a triumph. The scene in which Stephen outwits Herbert Pembroke has the kind of stength that one finds in *A Passage to India* and the better parts of *Maurice*. Here, without any false heroics, we are made aware that Rickie's sacrifice has borne fruit (if only in his final long short story) and that Mrs Failing has been proved wrong. The one brother has laid down his life for the other. Forster had already referred to Castor and Pollux in 'The Point of It'; and once again we find that life can only be had at the cost of death. Instead of Philip Herriton's death-in-life we are presented with Rickie's life-in-death. In neither case is there a completely affirmative resolution of the novelist's dilemma.

So much for the novel's constituents. One can see them as a programme for a characteristic novel of the period, coming to a tragic but cathartic conclusion, the best that a homosexual novelist could at that time offer. And there are indeed occasions when Forster pulls the stops out so that the novel invites such a reading. But the eccentricities of technique, the narrative innovations, constantly refute that particular approach.

The abrupt handling of violent events is a case in point. 'Gerald died that afternoon' – the opening of Chapter 5 is famous – or notorious: the words seem written, coming when they do, with a smack of the lips. The casual way in which death is introduced into the novel serves as a reminder that the eternal verities lie elsewhere, and rebukes our exclusive concern with clock time; but it may also be that Forster's recorded contempt for the story as such – 'a low, atavistic form' – leads him to play tricks on the reader. 'You want a story? You shall have one.' But in doing so he risks a sense of triviality. The death of Gerald, for example, apart from its inherent unlikelihood, is an uneasy mixture of hard and soft. The hard – Agnes riding down to the football field on her bicycle and then, after Gerald is dead, riding home again, bowing to her acquaintance as she goes – is excellent; the soft, the deathbed scene, does not ring true.

As in all the novels there is plenty of authorial comment. But here it serves as an alienation device: it is as though Forster were cautioning us not to get too involved, not to care about Rickie too much; and he has himself confessed that 'sometimes I went wrong deliberately, as if the spirit of anti-literature had jogged my elbow'.[3] He speaks about his hero not as an author usually speaks about a character he has invented, but almost as a social worker might, or a tutor; at times, even, like a governess.

He is, of course, absurdly young – not twenty-one – and he will be engaged to be married at twenty-three. He has no knowledge of the world; for example, he thinks that if you do not want money you can give it to friends who do. He believes in humanity because he knows a dozen decent people. He believes in women because he has loved his mother.   (Ch. 7)

We are being invited to sit in judgement upon Rickie; or, if not to judge, then at least to take up a superior attitude towards him. It is certainly easy to do so: his surrender to the Pembrokes is galling for the sympathetic reader. In Alan Wilde's phrase, 'Rickie's perceptions have become slovenly.'⁴ His rejection is accomplished in the truly alarming Chapter 23. What makes it alarming is its combination of some of the finest, most intense writing that Forster ever produced with a sudden dismissive standing back that reveals a despair even more total than Rickie's own. In it Rickie and Agnes have a quarrel over Stephen which finally estranges them. It opens with the remark about Agnes, quoted earlier, 'She had got over the tragedy: she got over everything.' The dialogue between them is sharp, to the point, and well written: the difference between their two outlooks on life is suggested when Rickie cries out that 'the lie we acted has ruined our lives'. Forster comments that 'She looked in bewilderment at the well-appointed room.' But, as the scene nears its climax, the author intervenes with obliterating effect: 'Her reply need not be quoted. It was the last time he attempted intimacy. And the remainder of their conversation, though long and stormy, is also best forgotten.' Let other pens dwell on guilt and misery? But the tone here is Mrs Herriton's; and though one presumes that a kind of double irony is being attempted (it is a habit of Forster's) it has a disabling effect. But then we are taken back into the novel, with an account of Rickie's tormented thoughts about his marriage and about Stephen, movingly and truly given. However, this terminates with the words 'Henceforward he deteriorates.' The effect is chilling, and chilling in the wrong way. The succeeding words make a play for compassion: 'Let those who censure him suggest what he should do. He has lost the work that he loved, his friends, and his child. He remained conscientious and decent, but the spiritual part of him proceeded towards ruin.' But the remark about deterioration has done its work: Rickie has been abandoned by his creator, dropped from being the child of his imagination and turned into a case history. Or is it that the author himself has not got the imaginative strength to plumb any deeper the tragedy he has uncovered? For *The Longest Journey* sounds at times as though it were being told by Forster to himself rather than to his public. The alienation devices seem to be so much wincing away from pain. Forster's message may be the same as that of Lawrence; but he lacks Lawrence's hammer-and-tongs, no-holds-barred method of setting it forth. (But, on the other hand, let it not be forgotten that he was only twenty-seven when he wrote the book.)

Ironically, one of the warmest tributes to Rickie's character ('lovable . . . absolutely dear') came from 'Elizabeth',[5] the Gräfin von Arnim, on whose character a good deal of Mrs Failing's appears to have been based; and Rickie does attract by virtue of a certain appealing helplessness and muddle in practical affairs, and of the very real and high-spirited idealism of his Cambridge days. Indeed, the novel can also be read as a testing of that idealism: Rickie, lacking Ansell's intellectual toughness and emotional restraint, carries his view of life into a world implacably opposed to it. His greatest weakness is 'an inherent tendency to view his experience symbolically rather than realistically'.[6] A lesser writer would have made him strong or noble: Forster, however, loads the dice against him from the start. The testing is to be total.

That it is Rickie's idealism that is his undoing does not discredit it, otherwise *The Longest Journey* could not properly be called a tragedy; but the way in which the author's concern for him turns into anger argues a degree of personal involvement that imperils the novel's standing as a work of art: Forster at times seems angry with a parent's anger with the child that has run itself into danger. Certainly Rickie the muddler is more convincing than Rickie the idealist; but this is a matter of expression rather than of action. Forster's comedy is written with more confidence than are the more overtly 'significant' passages – as was to continue to be the case until *A Passage to India*. Crucial in this respect is Rickie's vision of the lovers. The sharply observed, somewhat brutal account of what he sees is followed by a lyrical evocation of his emotional response.

Music flowed past him like a river. He stood at the springs of creation and heard the primeval monotony. Then an obscure instrument gave out a little phrase. The river continued unheeding. The phrase was repeated, and a listener might know it was a fragment of the Tune of tunes. Nobler instruments accepted it, the clarionet protected, the brass encouraged, and it rose to the surface to the whisper of violins. In full unison was Love born, flame of the flame, flushing the dark river beneath him and the virgin snows above. His wings were infinite, his youth eternal; the sun was a jewel on his finger as he passed it in benediction over the world. Creation, no longer monotonous, acclaimed him, in widening melody, in brighter radiances. Was Love a column of fire? Was he a torrent of song? Was he greater than either – the touch of a man on a woman?   (Ch. 3)

If the passage is meant seriously, then it is in full keeping with Rickie's own emotional state; it is certainly of its period, complete with alliteration, poetic inversions and the rhetorical questions characteristic of the early Forster. But if it is meant seriously then the next paragraph jars with greater effect than if it were written in mockery: 'It was the merest accident that Rickie had not been disgusted. But this he could not know.' Had the musical passage been a satire, the let-down would provoke a snigger; if it is taken seriously we have a typical Forsterian ambivalence. Everything depends on the tone and how we read it. But in any case the vision is apprehended wrongly. Instead of accepting it as a pointer to something beyond itself, Rickie equates image with reality, and thus creates an idol. He is voyeuristically excited by the lovers, but especially by the sadistic Gerald. His marriage is thus corrupt from the start, and can be seen as a participation in, not a refutation of, the life that Gerald represents. He steps into the bully's shoes, and it is thus psychologically appropriate that Agnes should subdue him; he has already, in his blind romanticism, gone over to the enemy.

Rickie's idealism causes havoc not only in his own life but also in the lives of those around him; like Portia in Elizabeth Bowen's *The Death of the Heart* (1938) he is a destructive innocent. But the Pembrokes get over it, and Agnes marries again – is it a Forsterian joke that she should become a Mrs Keynes? – and Rickie's personal tragedy is swallowed up in the daily affairs of the world he had misunderstood. All the same, the sense of sheer waste at the end is overwhelming, at least where Rickie is concerned. It is as though Forster were able to imagine a happy solution only for the demon boy turned brother, and not yet for his hero. And in *The Longest Journey* the way in which he appears to fall out of love with that hero gives the book its peculiarly tense and jittery quality. Clearly it was designed as a more positive and significant statement than its predecessor; and yet Rickie's sacrifice strikes one as a more literary solution than the impasse reached by Philip Herriton. Forster indeed is at no pains to prove it otherwise. If Rickie has saved Stephen it remains true that he died comfortless; there is no attempted softening of that fact. It is a book written, one senses, out of great pain; and its very vitality, its bitterness and moral penetration justify Lionel Trillings' comment that 'it does not so much fall apart as fly apart; the responsive reader can be conscious not of an inadequate plan or of a defect in structure but rather of the too-much steam that blows up the boiler'.[7]

Never a favourite with the general run of his readers, the book was understandably a favourite of Forster's own, for there is more of himself in this tragedy than in its more satisfying but cynical predecessor. As a moral fable it remains, in its particular context and terms of reference, a work of unique and continuing interest. Its ambiguous attitude to its unhappy hero exemplifies to perfection the crippling restrictions that social attitudes imposed upon a homosexual writer even when he was attempting to bring to that society a positive and enlarging vision. In its different way and different circumstances, *The Longest Journey* was as much a literary casualty as *The Rainbow* was to be. In this instance too, the relation of Forster to Lawrence is a closer one than may at first appear.

7 *A Room with a View*

In *A Room with a View* Forster takes up the fragments contrasting Italy and England which are found in the early 'Lucy novels'
and brings them to a successful conclusion. This time the Italian
world ensures victory and not defeat; but the victory is won by a
narrow margin. *Where Angels Fear to Tread* had followed a
European tradition rather than an English one when it subjected
its hero to a process of humiliation and self-scrutiny as a result of
his moving from a northern clime to the warmth and freedom of
the Mediterranean world: André Gide's *The Immoralist* (1902)
and Thomas Mann's *Death in Venice* (1903) show the encounter
between the two civilisations as being, in homosexual terms,
devastating. But Forster, by his use of indirection and disguise,
keeps his tone light and his horizons wide. Less tormented by
guilt than Gide (or, for that matter, than Proust), he is not
disposed to follow Mann's version of the homosexual condition
as a symbol of artistic sterility. Rather, he now makes use of the
particular social shifts and dodges attendant on the condition to
evoke a comic world in which his heroine's choice between life
and death can be presented without portentousness. The novel
represents a rejection of self-pity, and a choice of limitation in the
name of a greater freedom. The evasion of tragedy may make
this novel seem more lightweight than its predecessors; but
comedy is no less significant a vehicle for moral evaluation than
is its counterpart, and *A Room with a View* in fact offers a more
rounded picture of the moral dilemmas that were Forster's main
concern than any story he had as yet written.

It is probably his most well-liked novel, perhaps because
(with the dubious exception of *Maurice*) it is the only one to have
a happy ending. It tells the story of Lucy Honeychurch, a young
woman as delightful and innocent as her name suggests. Lucy is
on holiday in Italy with her middle-aged cousin, Charlotte
Bartlett. At a *pensione* in Florence they encounter an eccentric
English couple, the Emersons, father and son. Lucy and George

Emerson are drawn together, following a murder in the Piazza Signoria; and later on, at a picnic, he gives her a kiss. Miss Bartlett sees this. She carries her off to Rome, where Lucy becomes engaged to the aesthetic and rather priggish Cecil Vyse. The main parties are then reassembled in Surrey, where the Honeychurches live, and the Emersons rent a house in the same neighbourhood, so that Lucy and George are once again thrown together. He kisses her again. She breaks off her engagement to Cecil, but still refuses to accept George. She is finally brought to her senses by old Mr Emerson, and the pair are married, although the marriage remains unpopular with her family and friends.

The plot, then, is far more simple than those of the book's two predecessors: far more of the action is determined by the interplay of character, operated on by chance events that are upshots of personality and environment. The two early 'Lucy' fragments show that the Italian scenes were to be part of the novel from the start ('Old Lucy' is indeed all Italian); and both texts are written with much of the author's later sparkle and vivacity.[1] But Forster did not find himself able to accomplish the resolution of the situation which he had devised in them, the situation which is resolved in differing ways in his first two published novels: that of the conflict between the heart and the conventions as known by someone who tries to adhere to both. In 'New Lucy' the young author, compulsively it would seem, kills off the demon boy who is to be the only possible rescuer (for the George Emerson character plays that role). In the final version the boy is himself rescued, but in the nick of time. One reason for this may be that the central character is a girl: a happy solution is thus socially permissible.

The book has great charm. The Tunbridge Wells world, so to call it, is made matter for indulgent comedy; but the points are not thereby blunted. One notable feature of the book is the strongly feminine atmosphere: Lucy and her mother, Charlotte Bartlett (perhaps Forster's greatest comic creation), the Miss Alans, Miss Lavish, Minnie Beebe – they pervade the book, and even Cecil and Mr Beebe, the (at first) friendly clergyman, seem to belong to this world rather than to the one normally associated with men. The two Emersons also, in their curious domestic relationship, have something female about them. The book has a storm-in-a-teacup quality.

It is not, therefore, the female world as such which is menacing; and there are no Mrs Herritons or Mrs Failings in it (Miss Bartlett is a different matter altogether). But the world of 'ladies' is here seen from the inside: it is the room from which there is no view. But it is subject to much merry scrutiny. Unlike Ronald Firbank, Forster did not find women funny as such;[2] but what does amuse him is female propriety – at any rate in this novel (it will be a different matter when we come to *Maurice*). But even in 'Old Lucy' he has what for him is a ribald scene in which the Emerson character, a Mr Jacobs, scandalises the *pensione*'s dinner table by repeated (the word seems appropriate) mention of his stomach. And in the final version it is the appearance of 'ladies' by the woodland pool where George, Lucy's brother Freddie and Mr Beebe are bathing which provides one of the comic highlights of the book.

Comedy is used purposefully here; as Frederick Crews observes, whereas in most books of this kind 'the humour derives from the failure of certain characters to fulfil their social roles . . . here the comic characters are precisely those who take society too seriously'.[3] Cecil, in bringing the Emersons to Windy Corner 'In the interests of the Comic Muse and of Truth', deliberately cites George Meredith; and in true Meredithian manner he is hoist with his own petard, a minor Sir Willoughby Patterne. But Cecil and Meredith are right: comedy does in this instance lead to truth.

Among the victims of Forster's satire are the clergy, who come out badly in this novel, being represented as both snobbish and repressive. Forster puts his finger on that festering self-punishment which leads to the worship of sorrow, and of which Mr Borenius in *Maurice* is such a frightening example. Opposed to such nullity is old Mr Emerson's philosophy, a philosophy which, as enunciated by him, has dated rather: as Rose Macaulay observed, 'he talks too much and is too much soaked in the publications of the Rationalist Press Association and perhaps in the more symbolic pictures of G. E. Watts'.[4] But P. N. Furbank suggests that he is probably based on the character of Samuel Butler, about whom Forster was, in 1914, to consider writing a book.[5] Mr Emerson's philosophy, like Butler's, hits at Christianity; but it is also opposed to the fashionable *fin-de-siècle* world-weariness of Housman. (George, indeed, is originally introduced as a victim of 'Shropshire Lad' melancholia.)

We know that we come from the winds, and that we shall return to them; that all life is perhaps a knot, a tangle, a blemish in the eternal smoothness. But why should this make us unhappy? Let us rather love one another, and work and rejoice. I don't believe in this world sorrow.   (Ch. 2)

Mr Emerson has indeed just quoted Housman, and this is significant, for here we have a poet whose pessimism and nostalgia is largely motivated and propelled by his suppressed homo-eroticism. Forster's brother figures and ideal friends are not so far from the lads of Ludlow fair. But even as early as this we find Forster fighting back towards self-acceptance and self-fulfilment. Nostalgia and self-pity are not for him.

Self-acceptance is reached through delight: such is the comic vision in this book. All the small details work towards it; even a minor character such as Miss Alan contributes towards the total vision. Her account of Miss Lavish's novel-writing propensities prepares us for their later appearance in Lucy's story; but it is also a piece of delicious satire in itself, one which furthers the good spirits which pervade the book to such cleansing effect.

It was a novel – and I am afraid, from what I can gather, not a very nice novel. It is so sad when people who have abilities misuse them, and I must say they nearly always do. Anyhow, she left it almost finished in the Grotto of the Calvary at the Capuccini Hotel at Amalfi while she went for a little ink. She said, 'Can I have a little ink, please?' But you know what Italians are, and meanwhile the Grotto fell roaring on to the beach, and the saddest thing of all is that she cannot remember what she has written. The poor thing was very ill after it, and so got tempted into cigarettes. It is a great secret, but I am glad to say that she is writing another novel. She told Teresa and Miss Pole the other day that she had got up all the local colour – this novel is to be about modern Italy; the other was historical – but that she could not start till she had an idea. First she tried Perugia for an inspiration, then she came here – this must on no account get round. And so cheerful through it all! I cannot help thinking that there is something to admire in every one, even if you do not approve of them.   (Ch. 3)

This is like Mrs Forrester in *Cranford*; was that naming of Miss

Pole a piece of unconscious association?

Even for one of Forster's, the novel is remarkable for its multifaceted narrative. The following passage is typical in its evocation of everyday pleasantness and in the way in which the author brings his readers into the party while at the same time unobtrusively conveying a good deal of information. The Miss Alans are proposing to rent a house near Windy Corner where the Honeychurches live.

Playing bumble-puppy with Minnie Beebe, niece to the rector, and aged thirteen – an ancient and most honourable game, which consists in striking tennis-balls high into the air, so that they fall over the net and immoderately bounce; some hit Mrs Honeychurch; others are lost. The sentence is confused, but the better illustrates Lucy's state of mind, for she was trying to talk to Mr Beebe at the same time.

'Oh, it has been such a nuisance – first he, then they – no one knowing what they wanted, and everyone so tiresome.'

'But they really are coming now,' said Mr Beebe. 'I wrote to Miss Teresa a few days ago – she was wondering how often the butcher called, and my reply of once a month must have impressed her favourably. They are coming. I heard from them this morning.'

'I shall hate those Miss Alans!' Mrs Honeychurch cried. 'Just because they're old and silly one's expected to say "How sweet:" I hate their "if"-ing and "but"-ing and "and"-ing. And poor Lucy – serve her right – worn to a shadow.'

Mr Beebe watched the shadow springing and shouting over the tennis court. Cecil was absent – one did not play bumble-puppy when he was there.

'Well, if they are coming – No, Minnie, not Saturn.' Saturn was a tennis-ball whose skin was partially unsown. When in motion his orb was encircled by a ring. 'If they are coming, Sir Harry will let them move in before the twenty-ninth, and he will cross out the clause about whitewashing the ceilings, because it made them nervous, and put in the fair wear and tear one. That doesn't count. I told you not Saturn.'

'Saturn's all right for bumble-puppy,' cried Freddy, joining them. 'Minnie, don't you listen to her.'

'Saturn doesn't bounce.'

'Saturn bounces enough.'

'No, he doesn't.'

'Well, he bounces better than the Beautiful White Devil.'

'Hush, dear,' said Mrs Honeychurch.

'But look at Lucy – complaining of Saturn, and all the time's got the Beautiful White Devil in her hand, ready to plug it in. That's right, Minnie, go for her – get her over the shins with the racquet – get her over the shins!'

Lucy fell; the Beautiful White Devil rolled from her hand.

Mr Beebe picked it up, and said: 'The name of this ball is Vittoria Corrombona, please.' But his correction passed unheeded.   (Ch. 10)

It has been necessary to quote at such length in order to demonstrate Forster's command of what might be called the musicalities of narrative. In its inconsequence and delicate allusiveness the passage anticipates the experiments of Firbank; but the 'confused' sentence has stayed Forster's own, the alienation device being employed here to induce a feeling of intimacy and participation. And the subsequent interjections and the introduction of apparently irrelevant detail and the joke about Vittoria Corrombona and the clergyman's propriety of speech – all these things amount to a narrative technique that appeals to the half-conscious process of association, one which attempts to capture not only what happens, but how it happens. It is a style peculiar to Forster.

– Indeed, the musical quality of life is itself a recurring theme in the novel. Lucy's one great form of self-expression is the piano; it is through her playing that we, and certain characters in the book, can sense what she is truly feeling. Forster remarks that 'she loved to play on the side of Victory' – a welcome change from the tone of the two preceding novels. When her spirits are low, and the falseness of her position with regard to George troubles her, she plays Schumann; when inwardly responding she plays Beethoven – of whom Forster was to write memorably in *Howards End*.

'Now some Beethoven,' called Cecil, when the querulous beauty of the music had died. She shook her head and played Schumann again. The melody rose, unprofitably magical. It broke; it was resumed broken, not marching once from the cradle to the grave. The sadness of the incomplete – the sadness that is often Life, but should never be Art – throbbed in its disjected phrases, and made the nerves of the audience throb.   (Ch. 11)

The collocation of inward and outward is exact; moreover, it brings Lucy herself the more alive for us.

Victory and defeat: the story is that of Lucy's deliverance from her enemies. Strangely enough, in this most lighthearted of the novels, the enemies are more in evidence than in its predecessors, and are handled with greater subtlety and skill. On the periphery are Mr Eager, the stiff-backed, rancorous chaplain to the English congregation in Florence; and Miss Lavish, the lady novelist. (They have a surprising pair of names for the enemy to possess.) Mr Eager is conventional enough, snobbery, propriety and narrow-mindedness incarnate: the comedy here is straight satire, laced with anger. Appropriately he is outwitted, defeated by Italy, that happy chaos which, in Forster's imaginative terminology, is the state of grace.

Miss Lavish, because she professes to understand that state of grace, is more dangerous; but her bohemianism is a sham. She is an 'anti-Forsyte' and yet another of those mischief-making ladies who, in Forster's book, write books. But this time the woman writer precipitates not catastrophe but a happy ending. The use of Miss Lavish's novel to expose Lucy's meeting with George was part of the novel from its inception, and 'New Lucy' makes pleasant use of it.

In the inner ring the enemies are Cecil Vyse and Charlotte Bartlett; but somewhere between the two rings of enemies is the enigmatic figure of Mr Beebe. He is one of Forster's most penetrating studies, and essential to the particular atmosphere the book engenders. In him the cautious, self-punishing homosexual consciousness that acquiesces in the verdict of religion and society finds an embodiment familiar in other terms, that of the bachelor with an old mother who disguises his real desires under the cloak of celibacy.

His belief in celibacy, so reticent, so carefully concealed beneath his tolerance and culture, now came to the surface and expanded like some delicate flower. 'They that marry do well, but they that refrain do better.' So ran his belief, and he never heard that an engagement was broken off but with a slight feeling of pleasure.   (Ch. 18)

Jeffrey Meyers, in a generally unfriendly account of Forster's homosexual stories, suggests that Mr Beebe has in fact fallen in love with George during the bathing scene, and that his later change of character is the result of jealousy.[6] Certainly, if the pun be permitted (Forster encourages it), that character has a sting in it, for all its participation in the aptly named Honeychurch world: Mr Beebe embodies the poisonous self-rejection from which the novel seeks to break away. Whatever the personal implications for Forster himself, this attitude is firmly refuted; but Mr Beebe's intransigence remains, like the disapproval of Mrs Honeychurch, as an irreconcilable note in the final resolution, a miniature Cordelia's death to salt what might otherwise be too bland an optimism.

Charlotte Bartlett, on the other hand, surprises us in a different way. As an embodiment of all the muddle and misery of Sawstonian unselfishness she is unsurpassed in Forster's fiction. She is just the kind of person who can be relied on to arrive by the wrong train.

'I shall never forgive myself,' said Miss Bartlett, who kept on rising from her seat, and had to be begged by the united company to remain. 'I have upset everything. Bursting in on young people! But I insist on paying for my cab up. Grant me that, at any rate.'   (Ch. 14)

The ability here to combine the discomfort caused by accusation with the discomfort caused by guilt is typical: Miss Bartlett is of those who, having denied her own desires, exists in a permanent state of fermenting obliquity. In the earlier versions she is more malign; and it is a measure of the resolute optimism of *A Room with a View* that she is given a second chance. Essentially she embodies a criticism of the 'aesthetic' attitude to life that elsewhere Forster has handled very much in its own terms. To Miss Bartlett 'beauty and delicacy were the same thing', and the consequence of such a view in her own life as well as that of others is a deadly one.

One says 'her own life' not only in terms of her active presence in the book. The hint that in her past there has been a denial similar to the one that Lucy makes of George is substantiated not only at the end, with Lucy's supposition that Charlotte may have unconsciously willed the marriage, but at Lucy's darkest hour, when she pretends that she does not love him. While Truth says that she must reject Cecil, Propriety says that she must not accept George. This muddle gives rise to one of the author's most formidable sermons.

> [Lucy] gave up trying to understand herself, and joined the vast armies of the benighted, who follow neither the heart nor the brain, and march to their destiny by catch-words. The armies are full of pleasant and pious folk. But they have yielded to the only enemy that matters – the enemy within. They have sinned against passion and truth, and vain will be their strife after virtue. As the years pass, they are censured. Their pleasantry and their piety show cracks, their wit becomes cynicism, their unselfishness hypocrisy; they feel and produce discomfort wherever they go. They have sinned against Eros and Pallas Athene, and not by any heavenly intervention, but by the ordinary course of nature, those allied deities will be avenged.   (Ch. 17)

The words, heightened rhetorically though they are, carry the ring of absolute conviction. What follows is evidently meant to bear equal weight: 'Lucy entered this army when she pretended to George that she did not love him, and pretended to Cecil that she loved no one. The night received her, as it had received Miss Bartlett thirty years before.'

The precison of that last statement would seem to refer to some such specific choice as Lucy now has to make; and it implies that Lucy's own guess at the end of the novel concerning her cousin's motives is no idle piece of sentimentality. It is a courageous affirmation, implying a law of life that can work even through the subconscious.

The aesthetic fallacy in its purest form is caught in Cecil Vyse – who is possibly a self-punishing self-portrait. However, Forster is more merciful to him than he is to Rickie Elliot, even if he also exposes him more relentlessly.

> 'I count myself a lucky person,' he concluded. 'When I'm in London I feel I could never live out of it. When I'm in the country I feel the same about the country. After all, I do

believe that birds and trees and the sky are the most wonderful things in life, and that the people who live amongst them must be the best. It's true that in nine cases out of ten they don't seem to notice anything. The country gentleman and the country labourer are each in their way the most depressing of companions. Yet they may have a tacit sympathy with the workings of Nature which is denied to us of the town. Do you feel that, Mrs Honeychurch?'

Mrs Honeychurch started and smiled. She had not been attending. Cecil, who was rather crushed on the front seat of the victoria, felt irritable, and determined not to say anything interesting again.   (Ch. 9)

Cecil here unconsciously parodies the sloppy nature-writing and thought that were to be prevalent in the years to come; but behind him looms the nobler shade of Meredith. Indeed, the presence of Meredith haunts the second part of the novel and its Surrey landscapes; and, as we have seen, Cecil invokes the Meredithian spirit of comedy to his own cost when he substitutes the Emersons for the Miss Alans in the cottage by the church. Forster may even be satirising, if not Meredith, then the Meredith cult. But Cecil's lovemaking in the wood anticipates that of Mr Wilcox at Swanage in *Howards End*. He asks Lucy if he may kiss her and receives the reply,

'Of course you may, Cecil. You might before. I can't run at you, you know.'

At that supreme moment he was conscious of nothing but absurdities. Her reply was inadequate. She gave such a businesslike lift to her veil. As he approached her he found time to wish that he could recoil. As he touched her, his gold pince-nez became dislodged and was flattened between them.

This absurd encounter takes place near the Sacred Lake – dried to a puddle before the rains fill it for George's naked bathe. It must be confessed that it is all too typical of a Forster love scene: he may believe in passion but he prefers not to write about it. The approach to a romantic moment makes him self-conscious, and, like Cecil, he backs away. His very definition of passion in part explains this: it would fit badly into the kind of novel he chose to write, for it 'should forget civility and consideration and all the other curses of a refined nature. Above all, it should never ask for leave where there is a right of way.' Cecil too is aware of this, but can only meet the problem in his (Meredithian) imagination: 'He recast the scene. Lucy was standing flower-like by the water; he rushed up and took her in his arms; she rebuked him, permitted him, and revered him ever after for his manliness. For he believed that women revere men for their manliness.' The whole Edwardian male and female role-playing falls flat with that remark.

But Cecil is not without redeeming features: if he were, he would not be so dangerous an enemy to Lucy's happiness. Prig though he is, his creator understands him, and we have the sense of a character known from within and not one merely set up for rejection. But that Lucy should in the end reject him is inevitable, for he too constitutes a room without a view.

Lucy's action is more positively understood as a refusal of Cecil than as an acceptance of George. Forster presents the novel as being concerned with emancipation (it appeared while the suffragette disturbances were nearing their peak) and Lucy does in her quiet way stand for woman; as early as Chapter 4, Forster is placing her in this context. Of woman he says,

In her heart there are springing up strange desires. She too is enamoured of heavy winds, and vast panoramas, and green expanses of the sea. She has marked the kingdom of this world, how full it is of wealth, and beauty, and war – a radiant crust, built around the central fires, spinning towards the receding heavens. Men, declaring that she inspires them to it, move joyfully over the surface, having the most delightful meetings with other men, happy, not because they are masculine, but because they are alive. Before the show breaks up she would like to drop the august title of the Eternal Woman, and go there as her transitory self.

There is more than a touch of Virginia Woolf at her most archly lyrical about this. Lucy fits into, rather than forms, the picture it presents; she has to fight for the right to know and be herself. And, as with Philip Herriton, the struggle takes place as a result of contact with the South and a radical questioning of the tenets of a middle-class English upbringing.

Though inclined to get muddled, Lucy responds positively to

Italy. Not so Cecil. Where Lucy 'felt that there was no one whom she might not get to like', 'Italy had quickened Cecil, not to tolerance, but to irritation.' Forster is very acute here, in his anatomising of a certain kind of rebellion, the rebellion that is, as it were, away from something old, rather than into something new. 'He saw that the local society [of Surrey] was narrow, but, instead of saying, "Does this very much matter?" he rebelled, and tried to substitute for it the society he called broad' (Ch. 10). So he is unable to fit into Lucy's home world, which Forster so affectionately re-creates. 'He did not realize that Lucy had consecrated her environment by the thousand little civilities that create a tenderness in time, and that though her eyes saw its defects, her heart refused to despise it entirely.' Lucy can bridge the gap between the two worlds, and in so doing is able to find her way to George, who unites them.

George himself is rather an enigma; he is shadowily conceived, and even his intellectual struggles with the world around him are left undeveloped. Strong, vulnerable, melancholic, articulate at need, he seems to be a mass of contradictions: only in relation to Lucy does he exist at all. One thing is supremely important about him: that, where Charlotte talks about the kiss among the violets, he keeps silent. It is the decisive difference between them where Lucy is concerned. Certainly he is anything but a conqueror, and in him the roles of demon boy and anti-heroic hero are united. It is his vulnerability which helps to win Lucy's heart. Although to one of her upbringing 'the weakness of men was a truth unfamiliar', 'his awkwardness went straight to her heart: men were not gods after all, but as human and as clumsy as girls; even men might suffer from unexplained desires, and need help' (Ch. 15). This is a point that all Forster's novels were to make. His own sense of inferiority in the eyes of the contemporary Edwardian male ideal leads him to anticipate a society no longer dominated by such rigid and artificial sexual polarities.

George, then, is the solution of Lucy's sense of her own independent womanhood. This is indicated by the very delicacy and slightness of their love-making. Never before, one is tempted to say, was so much fuss made about a kiss upon the cheek. But this may well be the point: the smallness of the caress is unimportant, it is the drive behind it which matters. George, unlike Cecil, did not wait to be asked, for he knew that the way was clear – as does the reader, for Lucy comes upon the slope of violets in much the same confusion of spirit as, in *A Passage to India*, Adela Quested was to wander into the Marabar cave. Lucy's moment of truth, however, has a happier outcome.

But only just: the novel generates an altogether new kind of suspense over the well-worn 'Will she, won't she?' situation; one might call it a Trollopian novel keyed to a higher pitch of awareness. We are, for all the smallness of scale, made to feel that what we are being presented with is a matter of life and death. Old Mr Emerson's final plea is properly eloquent.

> Take an old man's word: there's nothing worse than a muddle in all the world. It is easy to face Death and Fate, and the things that sound so dreadful. It is on my muddles that I look back with horror – on the things that I might have avoided. We can help one another but little. I used to think I could teach young people the whole of life, but I know better now, and all my teaching of George has come down to this: beware of muddle. Do you remember in that church, when you pretended to be annoyed with me and weren't? Do you remember before, when you refused the room with the view? Those were muddles – little, but ominous – and I am fearing that you are in one now.   (Ch. 19)

So Lucy accepts her room with a view, at the cost of estrangement from her friends: even in this sunniest of his books Forster does not withhold a morsel of gall. And if on the third attempt he manages to present a convincing deliverance from the world that has defeated Philip Herriton and Rickie Elliot, it is partly as a result of transposing the sex of his hero. The novel may be said to get away with it rather than to triumph. Forster circumnavigates and outflanks the enemy, avoiding a direct confrontation with the powers of spiritual materialism. George and Lucy's very isolation at the end is telling. For if the novel solves the challenge of modern life in personal terms, there still remains the fact that there are other and competing claims to possess reality, contradictions inherent in the society of the day. It is to Forster's credit that he should have made the attempt, however unsuccessfully, to reconcile them in social terms through the unfolding of his next, longest and most ambitious novel to date, *Howards End*.

8   Howards End

The English country house makes frequent appearances in early-twentieth-century fiction. As the focus of Christian feudalism, a repository for artistic achievements, a symbol of continuity, it was an embodiment of traditional civilised ideals which lent itself to both nostalgia and defiance. The literary handling of it by Forster's contemporaries and their successors is varied and frequent. As Bladesover in Wells' *Tono-Bungay* (1909) for example, and as the Tolbrook of Joyce Cary's *To Be a Pilgrim* (1942), we find it used both to record and to assess the process of social change. In the novels of Lawrence, on the other hand, it tends to be an embodiment of social oppression – Shortlands in *Women in Love* (1920) and Wragby Hall in *Lady Chatterley's Lover* (1928) provide variants on this theme. Then there is the subject of class. We find it handled with chilling restraint in a novel which Forster much admired, Howard Overing Sturgis's *Belchamber* (1904); and it is frequently explored in the novels of John Galsworthy, where the various houses – for example, Worsted Keynes in *The Country House* (1907), Monkland Court in *The Patrician* (1911), Robin Hill in *The Forsyte Saga* (1906–21) – enable him to analyse the particular social qualities of the squirearchy, aristocrats and business men who inhabit them. Significantly, Robin Hill, built to order by the lawyer Soames Forsyte, is never inhabited by him at all, but passes to his ex-wife and her second husband, the artist Jolyon Forsyte: Forster was to make the same point about the alienation of the *nouveau riche* in his treatment of the Wilcoxes' Shropshire retreat, Oniton, in *Howards End*.

As the century proceeds, the great house, which, in the novels of Henry James, represents a moral and spiritual culture as well as a material one, dwindles to a doomed ideal – Evelyn Waugh's *Brideshead Revisited* (1945) being perhaps the most plangent and elaborate exploration of this theme, while the same process operates with more positive social connotations in novels such as E. Œ. Somerville's *The Big House at Inver* (1925) and Elizabeth Bowen's *The Last September* (1929), where the great Anglo-Irish mansions dominate narratives which culminate with their going up in flames. So, too, in Henry Green's *Loving* (1945) Castle Kinalty is continually threatened with burning; Poyntz Hall in *Between the Acts* (1941), Virginia Woolf's last and wartime novel, is another house that knows only a tenuous security. But the literary use of the country house as a symbol of continuity and permanence has been equally pervasive, as in *Parade's End* (1924–8) by Ford Madox Ford, and the early work of the Westmorland novelist Constance Holme. In each case the maintenance of the house involves the preservation of individual as well as social values, of a *home,* not just of wealth or inherited tradition. This approach to the country-house theme numbers *Howards End* among the earliest examples; and Forster himself was to describe the book as 'a hunt for a home'. It is a revealing comment.[1]

It is a characteristic of Forster that his symbolic house should be a small one: it is the continuity which it embodies that appeals to him – not its architecture, power or influence, still less any residual feudalism. For the big houses with their comforts and art treasures were largely financed by the rents their owners exacted from villagers and tenant farmers and urban slum-dwellers; and it would not have been like Forster to have sentimentalised that situation. But it was like him to make of his own childhood home, with all its personal associations, the focus of a novel which would examine the condition of England as he saw it, in terms of conflicting philosophies of which the only point of real agreement was, for widely differing motives, to keep that house in being. It was also like him to start with his house in the possession of the enemy, only to be restored to its true spiritual owners at the end. This most magisterial of the early novels may embody a personal dream. Forster's use of Rooks-nest in this way is a perfect example of that mythologising of his private life which makes him as a novelist so intimate and yet portentous.

II

Howards End was Forster's most ambitious novel to date: it is also his most controversial one. The coincidence of those two statements highlights the peculiar problems which the book raises for a critic: it provides a testing of the author's imaginative world as material for a novel of impersonal statement, the kind of novel that seems to aim at classic status. What has been essentially self-expression in its three predecessors now becomes a venture into more assured and more widespread comment on the world around him. It was a challenge to Forster's art in every sense, to its technique, its preoccupations, its relevance and scope.

Whatever else, the book did not meet the fate of many over-ambitious novels – the author was not told to go on writing the limited books which had earned him his first success. *Howards End* was much admired when it came out, and has been read and enjoyed as much as any of Forster's other novels. And critical praise of it has risen to great heights, Lionel Trilling, for instance, regarding it as his masterpiece and 'a work of full responsibility'.[2] Such a high estimate, however, is not only inaccurate but also misleading. It is in the book's failures as much as in its successes that its interest lies.

For all its characteristically casual opening the novel is carefully deployed. As early as 1910 Forster could foresee the challenge to liberal values constituted by the new age of international finance and competing nationalisms; and he met the challenge, again characteristically, not with defiance but with self-questioning. But in so doing he not only raised the dilemma: he also enacted it. In *Howards End* he presents himself with a situation with which his art was not as yet equipped to deal.

As with any major novel, it is possible to read *Howards End* in more than one way. As early as 1908 Forster had written in his diary, 'No more fighting, please, between the soul & the body, until they have beaten their common enemy the machine.'[3] On the face of it the novel concerns the competing claims of action and contemplation. The claims for priority in the building of modern civilisation are here embodied in the ways of life of two contrasting families. We are presented with two sisters of international, in this case Anglo-German, parentage. Margaret and

Helen Schlegel are independent and high-minded young women who live with their young brother Theobald (better known as Tibby – another example of Forster's intimacies) in a flat in London. Chance throws them into contact with a family named Wilcox – 'business people', so D. H. Lawrence called them.[4] Helen visits them at their country house, Howards End, the property of Mrs Wilcox. While there she falls in love with the younger son – and as quickly out again: the result is much embarrassment and fuss, recounted in Forster's highest comic manner. Later on, the two families come together again, and Margaret Schlegel makes friends with Mrs Wilcox, a friendship brought to a premature conclusion by the latter's death. Mrs Wilcox leaves behind her a written request that Howards End be given to Margaret; but the family ignores this. But later on, to Helen's dismay, Margaret and the widowed Henry Wilcox become engaged.

In the meantime the two sisters have befriended Leonard Bast, an impoverished clerk with a disreputable wife, and on Henry's casually given advice recommend him to change his place of work. The advice turns out to be bad; and, at the wedding of Henry's daughter Evie, Helen confronts him with the Basts, who, it turns out, are concerned with him in a still more unhappy way, Jacky Bast being his cast-off mistress. Despite this débâcle, Margaret and Henry marry, while Helen disappears abroad. Nine months later she turns up at Howards End, carrying Leonard's child. In a tumultuous climax Leonard is accidentally killed by Henry's elder son Charles (a reincarnation of Gerald Dawes) and the two sisters take over occupancy of Howards End, to care for Leonard's child and a broken Henry Wilcox.

On the reading suggested above, the novel traces the attempt of Margaret Schlegel through her marriage to reconcile the worlds of action and contemplation. The attempt fails, through the incurable muddle and materialism of the Wilcox point of view, which results in the lamentable affair of Leonard Bast. But the future is what matters, and that lies with Helen and Leonard's child.

So much for one line of interpretation. Another might see the novel as constructed round two contrasted personal relationships: that between Margaret and Henry, and that between Helen and Leonard. Now, the book appears to anticipate the structure of *Women in Love*. Margaret and Henry, like Ursula

Brangwen and Rupert Birkin, are working towards some sort of mutual accommodation; Helen and Leonard's affair is a matter of panic and loneliness, and ends in catastrophe. However, the comparison with Lawrence's novel is damaging for Forster, since passion is singularly absent from *Howards End*. In fact, both readings leave out of account the contrasting characters of the two sisters, a contrast which recalls that between Elinor and Marianne Dashwood in *Sense and Sensibility*. The distinction between them is the same: that between falsely romantic, self-indulgent passion and a reasoned, considerate affection resting on esteem. In *Howards End* the issue between the two sisters constitutes the moral fibre of the book; the Wilcoxes are presented too one-dimensionally to supply an adequate contrast.

'One may as well begin with Helen's letters to her sister.' That celebrated and most Forsterian opening is disingenuous. The letters are vital: they introduce us to the sisters' shared world, establish an intimacy between them and the reader which establishes their point of view as the one from which we are to follow all that happens after. But it is a dual point of view: the primary consciousness within the novel contains a tension. Gradually, however, Margaret's point of view takes over. The women's world of Wickham Place is the storehouse of liberal values; as against it, the Wilcox world has nothing to offer, for it ignores the personal life. Forster scarcely even tries to make anything of the Wilcoxes; and nowhere is his condemnation of the purely masculine world more total. But this means that the opposition of masculine and feminine, though presumably in intention central to the book, is not so in fact. The Wilcoxes are subservient to Margaret's evaluation, and to the changes in her attitude affected by two other women, Mrs Wilcox and Helen.

Few things are more characteristic of Forster's art than his handling of the character of Ruth Wilcox – unless it is his treatment of the not dissimilar character of Mrs Moore in *A Passage to India*. As a personality Mrs Wilcox is shadowy: indeed, she is singularly without that highly personalised, articulate individualisation which is what personality stands for in the Schlegel world. She cannot compete with that world (Forster's account of Margaret's luncheon party for her is one of his subtlest pieces of comedy), nor is she possessed of any especial mystical insight. What she does possess is common sense, and an intuitive feeling for other people's needs (as compared with formal perception: witness her incapacity over choosing Christmas presents). She is not 'good with people', as we say. But her name, Ruth, indicative of both faithfulness and exile, seems appropriate.

Her desire that Margaret should inherit Howards End, an assertion that there are such things as spiritual heirs, is avowedly at the heart of the book, which in this instance provides a significant modulation of Mrs Gereth's materialistic spirituality in Henry James's *The Spoils Of Poynton* (1896).[5] Forster is careful to stress the local particularity of the house, as if to counterbalance its symbolic significance: the name Howard is that of the family who once lived at Rooksnest, and 'End' is a Hertfordshire suffix, witness Mackery End in Lamb's *Esays of Elia*. (James's Covering End presumably comes from the same source.) The sense of locality is important in this novel, still more so than in its predecessors, and contrasts with the more formalised set-piece descriptions of Wiltshire in *The Longest Journey*. The very smallness of Howards End as a property renders it all the more domestic and vulnerable, menaced by Wilcox encroachments from within (Evie's rockery) and from without, as suburbia marches onward. Only the indigenous Miss Avery keeps guard with the sword, heir to the warriors buried in the earthworks of the Six Hills. The emotive presentation of Howards End is a strange mixture of the homely and the grandiloquent.

But at the start its effectiveness as a symbol is limited. The Wilcoxes dominate it; it is seen as part of their world, and the picture of Mrs Wilcox holding the wisp of hay is too slight, too contrived, to offset them.

She approached just as Helen's letter had described her, trailing noiselessly over the lawn, and there was actually a wisp of hay in her hands. She seemed to belong not to the young people and their motor, but to the house, and to the tree that overshadowed it. One knew that she worshipped the past, and that the instinctive wisdom the past can alone bestow had descended upon her – that wisdom to which we give the clumsy name of aristocracy. High born she might not be. But assuredly she cared about her ancestors, and let them help her. When she saw Charles angry, Paul frightened, and Mrs Munt in tears, she heard her ancestors say, 'Separate those human beings who will hurt each other most. The rest can wait.'   (Ch. 3)

The approach here is confusing. To whom does she seem remote? Aunt Juley? Hardly. Helen, presumably. But there is
nothing later in the novel to back up the impression on Helen's
part. And as an authorial comment the account of Mrs Wilcox is
overloaded and thus sentimental. The point Forster is making is
a valid one, and essential to the novel; but its introduction in this
manner seems ill conceived. That 'One knew' is perhaps the
jarring note. It induces the sense of a proffered superiority.

Indeed, it is less the house itself than the use to which the
author puts it that constitutes the symbol. The bequest of
Howards End to Margaret is, for the Wilcoxes, a situation
comparable to that with which Rickie Elliot is confronted when
Stephen's identity is revealed to him; but in this case, instead of a
moral choice such as Rickie is forced to make, Forster substitutes
a piece of characteristic authorial intervention.

> To them Howards End was a house: they could not know that
> to her it had been a spirit, for which she sought a spiritual heir.
> And – pushing one step further in these mists – may they not
> have decided even better than they supposed? Is it credible
> that the possessions of the spirit can be bequeathed at all? Has
> the soul offspring? A wych-elm tree, a vine, a wisp of hay with
> dew on it – can passion for such things be transmitted where
> there is no bond of blood? No; the Wilcoxes are not to be
> blamed. The problem is too terrific, and they could not even
> perceive a problem. No; it is natural and fitting that after the
> debate they should tear the note up and throw it on to their
> dining-room fire. The practical moralist may acquit them
> absolutely. He who strives to look deeper may acquit them –
> almost. For one hard fact remains. They did neglect a personal
> appeal. The woman who had died did say to them, 'Do this'
> and they answered, 'We will not.'   (Ch. 11)

The method of procedure here is skilful. The author seems at first
to take sides against himself, on account not only of his anti-
Wilcox bias but also of his invention of the bequest in the first
place; for when a novelist talks about his characters in this tone
he confers on them an autonomy that, paradoxically, seems to
make him responsible for what happens to them. At the same

time he claims to be more than a 'practical moralist'; and in terms of a deeper vision he indicates the limitation of that morality. We are led to condemn the Wilcoxes' action with the one part of our minds, while acquitting them with another. This is not muddle, as it has been defined in earlier novels, but an avoidance of it – if only by defining the nature of the problem of combining private and public standards of values. The whole chapter compares interestingly with the second one of *Sense and Sensibility*, most Forsterian of Jane Austen's novels. The Wilcoxes do have law and common sense on their side; but for all that the final qualification sounds a damning one. Henry James wrote in a letter to the French writer Paul Bourget that he had 'a thorough disbelief in any security with people who have no imagination. They are the objects, not the subjects, of imagination and it is not in their compass to *conceive* of anything whatever. They can only live their hard functional lives.'[6] This was written about the wealthy London upper class he portrays in *The Awkward Age* (1901), but it suits Forster's materialists just as well. They value Howards End not so much as a home as a piece of property.

The final takeover of the house by the sisters, with Henry Wilcox as a captive shattered inmate, has, in these terms, a kind of poetic justice: it is in keeping with Miss Avery's drastic action in unpacking the Schlegel furniture which has been stored there. Miss Avery herself, the countrywoman who has been Mrs Wilcox's friend, is an effective embodiment of the silent power of those forces in life of which the Wilcoxes take no account and cannot understand; and her appearance at the moment of Leonard's death has been prepared for by her earlier, arbitrary and rather eerie intrusions. But the almost mythological atmosphere which she imparts does not really consort with the social satire of the rest of the book; and the final solution constitutes more of a female victory in alliance than a resolution of the division between the two sisters. It is more an ending than a conclusion, and has little to do with the fundamental questions raised by the author in earlier novels. As David Cecil observes, Pan has been replaced by Ceres.[7] 'Replaced' is here the operative word.[8]

For Howards End has been the death of Leonard Bast, and it is he who provides the testing ground for the novel's delicate exploration of competing values. Leonard, like Rickie Elliot at Cadbury Rings, may be likened to the knight of the Grail who seeks the chalice of truth and beauty in art and nature; he is deprived of both by the well-meaning sisters. He is also, in another light, the kind of self-educated hero popularised at this time by H. G. Wells. But, whereas Kipps and Mr Polly are figures of high comedy, Leonard's role is tragic. It is also vital. He stands

> at the extreme verge of gentility. He was not in the abyss, but he could see it, and at times people whom he knew had dropped in, and counted no more. He knew that he was poor, and would admit it: he would have died sooner than confess any inferiority to the rich. This may be splendid of him.   (Ch. 6)

That 'may' should alert us to what follows: Forster is here treading deliberately on the toes of those who would sentimentalise poverty as such – which is why this particular chapter is prefaced by the flagrant irony of 'We are not concerned with the very poor. They are unthinkable, and only to be approached by the statistician or the poet.' The Wilcoxes and the Schlegels are neither of them these. And the Swiftian kind of flourish that the statement embodies is one that almost recoils upon its author. But he knows what he is doing. So, to return to Leonard Bast, he continues,

> But he was inferior to most rich people, there is not the least doubt of it. He was not as courteous as the average rich man, nor as intelligent, nor as healthy, nor as lovable. His mind and his body had been alike underfed, because he was poor, and because he was modern they were always craving better food . . . in his day the angel of Democracy had arisen, enshadowing the classes with leathern wings, and proclaiming, 'All men are equal – all men, that is to say, who possess umbrellas,' and so he was obliged to assert gentility, lest he slipped into the abyss where nothing counts, and the statements of Democracy are inaudible.

Forster wears his Fabianism with a difference: he seems here to have more affinities with the Wilde of *The Soul of Man under Socialism* than he does with more traditional radicals. But the Bernard Shaw of *Pygmalion* would have understood. Forster is

never muddled over materialism, and realises that to work for a
just society involves a reckoning with the way in which poverty
can corrupt as much as riches do – a distinction that is not always
to be found in the work of Dickens, for example. If the poor man
is fine and noble it is not because of his poverty, but in spite of it.

How precisely Forster realises the obstacles to Leonard's
freedom of thought and feeling (an understanding surely owing
to his teaching innumerable Leonards at the Working Men's
College) can be gauged by the scene where he tells the two sisters
of his night walk in the country. Fifteen years after *Jude the
Obscure* a great gulf still remains fixed between the self-
educated and those who have acquired their culture through
inheritance: Leonard wants to talk books, the ladies want to talk
life.

> 'But was the dawn wonderful?' asked Helen.
>   With unforgettable sincerity he replied, 'No.' The word flew
> again like a pebble from the sling. Down toppled all that had
> seemed ignoble or literary in his talk, down toppled tiresome
> R. L. S. and the 'love of the earth' and his silk top-hat. In
> the presence of these women Leonard had arrived, and he
> spoke with a flow, an exultation, that he had seldom
> known.   (Ch. 14)

There is considerable pathos in Leonard's attempts to articulate
not only what he *has* experienced, but what he is experiencing at
the very moment of telling it.

> 'Oh, hang it all! what's the good – I mean, the good of living in
> a room for ever? There one goes on day after day, same old
> game, same up and down to town, until you forget there is any
> other game. You ought to see once in a way what's going on
> outside, if it's only nothing particular after all.'
>   'I should just think you ought,' said Helen, sitting on the
> edge of the table.
>   The sound of a lady's voice recalled him from sincerity, and
> he said: 'Curious it should all come about from reading
> something of Richard Jefferies.'

Forster then proceeds to anatomise the post-Meredithian wash
of nature-writing and nature-worship, and through it to expose

the spiritual materialist's sentimentality where the country is concerned: in doing so he in fact frees us for a more discriminating and, beyond that, a less apologetic response to what we sense is there to be known and lived from. It is noteworthy that once again Surrey is the focus of attention.

> Borrow was imminent after Jefferies – Borrow, Thoreau and sorrow. R. L. S. brought up the rear, and the outburst ended in a swamp of books. No disrespect to these great names. The fault is ours, not theirs. They mean us to use them for sign-posts, and are not to blame if, in our weakness, we mistake the sign-posts for the destination. And Leonard had reached the destination. He had visited the county of Surrey when darkness had covered its amenities, and its cosy villas had re-entered ancient night. Every twelve hours this miracle happens, but he had troubled to go and see for himself. Within his cramped little mind dwelt something that was greater than Jefferies' books – the spirit that led Jefferies to write them; and his dawn, though revealing nothing but monotones, was part of the eternal sunrise that shows George Borrow Stonehenge.

This passage, however, is written from a Schlegel point of view; and the sermonette quality, so pleasing in other contexts, is heightened unpleasantly by that 'cramped little mind', saved here by no pre-emptive irony from sounding patronising. A passage like this reveals Forster in one of his maddening mixtures of acuity and needling primness.

Throughout the novel there is a fatal uncertainty of tone in the way he writes of Leonard. His very ability to see both points of view is in this instance his undoing, for to see Leonard both as he is in himself and as he appears to the Schlegels requires a more deliberate, elaborate, George Eliot-like approach than Forster's fictional methods usually allow. The result is an anger that seems to be directed less against the social and economic causes of Leonard's and Jacky's plight than against the pair of them for being in it. While the sentiment with which Forster writes about the couple is admirable, the tone is not. One senses a repressed aggression. Similarly, when Jacky is described as 'bestially stupid' (or, for that matter when Charles's wife Dolly is described as 'a rubbishy little creature and she knew it') the exasperation that leads to the remark issues not as compassion but as contempt. But, with Jacky, Forster is quite out of control: she is a figure of burlesque, and thrown about the novel like a rag doll, anatomised and rejected in a way quite out of keeping with the book's general intentions and philosophy. And her unreality affects our view of Leonard, so that in the end it is easier to view him from the Schlegel–Wilcox angle than from his own.

As a result it is impossible to imagine the encounter in the hotel at Oniton when Forster asks us to believe that Leonard becomes Helen's lover. That the scene is not presented directly is beside the point: much of Forster's action takes place off-stage. What does matter is that Leonard does not have a reality commensurate with that of Helen; and their actions in this instance seem more to have been decided for them by the author than to have been shared between themselves. And although Oliver Stallybrass's reminder that 'sympathy given and received can take an erotic turn'[9] says much for the plausibility of the idea, its actual presentation lacks conviction. Helen's child seems to be the result of a need for symbolism rather than the fruit of carnal lust.

The concluding scene with the child only serves, in fact, to confuse the issues between the two sisters. Helen, in her way, is as one-sided as the Wilcoxes: her impulsiveness leads to as much muddle as does their caution. Nowhere is this more apparent than in her financial dealings with the Basts. As naïve as Rickie is with Agnes and Gerald, she is a good deal more dangerous. After her disastrous visit to Oniton she goes off in remorse, not only leaving the penniless couple to settle the hotel bill but also taking their railway tickets with her. She then, by way of compensation, proposes to settle £5000 upon them – an act, in the final analysis, of contempt. But Leonard returns the cheque, and the Basts are evicted from their home and become untraceable. Helen, on the other hand,.

> had begun bungling with her money by this time, and had even sold out her shares in the Nottingham and Derby Railway. For some weeks she did nothing. Then she reinvested, and, owing to the good advice of her stockbrokers, became rather richer than she had been before.   (Ch. 30)

Were more of the novel couched in this tone, the conclusion might have been more persuasive than it is.

Instead, the need for a happy, pastoral ending, product

perhaps of Forster's dream of home, leaves the Schlegels in possession in a way that smacks more of main force than of poetic logic, and as though 'it is . . . of greater significance to connect Margaret and Ruth, than Margaret and Henry'.[10] Helen, who has really done more harm to the Basts than has Henry, is secure in Howards End: indeed it is she, rather than Margaret, who responds to the house's healing magic in the beautiful scene when the two sisters suffer a mutual estrangement following their reunion after Helen's flight. Moreover, her child is born in 'the central room of the nine' – the one that had been Forster's nursery. It is Helen too who creates for us the myth of the house when the novel opens; and she attains it not by penitence and faith, but by the natural processes of generation and motherhood. But this is to transpose the key in which the novel is told: one set of values is being substituted for another, and without due preparation. Even Margaret is left to reflect that 'She, who had never expected to conquer anyone, had charged straight through these Wilcoxes and broken up their lives': a very un-Schlegelian achievement. The final victory is too complete for the complexity of the issues raised. Perhaps Forster shared Tibby's attitude to the admittedly charming Helen, and might have been severer upon her than he is had she not been 'ceaselessly beautiful'.

But, despite its central flaw, *Howards End* is a wonderfully organised, rich and various novel. Characteristic of its method is the celebrated account of the concert in Chapter 5, which opens, 'It will be generally admitted that Beethoven's Fifth Symphony is the most sublime noise that has ever penetrated into the ear of man.'

How serious is that statement? It resounds; but resounding statements by Forster are always suspect and so are the people in his fiction who make them. But the use of the word 'noise' as distinct from the word 'sound' suggests an irony; and, without disrespect to a very great piece of music, one may question whether the author isn't here attempting a statement about popular taste rather than one about the music as such. Certainly the development of the passage directs our attention squarely on the audience.

Whether you are like Mrs Munt, and tap surreptitiously when the tunes come – of course, not so as to disturb the others – or like Helen, who can see heroes and shipwrecks in the music's flood; or like Margaret, who can only see the music; or like Tibby, who is profoundly versed in counterpoint, and holds the full score open upon his knee; or like their cousin, Fräulein Mosebach, who remembers all the time that Beethoven is 'echt Deutsch'; or like Fräulein Mosebach's young man, who can remember nothing but Fräulein Mosebach: in any case, the passion of your life becomes more vivid, and you are bound to admit that such a noise is cheap at two shillings.

These details not only serve as indicators of the characters (the difference between Margaret and Helen is particularly illuminating), but also suggest various ways of reading the novel. Mrs Munt (the girl's Aunt Juley) reads for the highlights in the story; Helen projects her own fantasies upon it; Tibby is the literary critic obsessed with technique; Fräulein Mosebach is the critic obsessed with ideology: so we may place them. (Fräulein Mosebach's young man is the same in every case, and one can be sure that Forster, unlike the majority of twentieth-century critics, commends him for it.) Margaret, however, who provides the book's central viewpoint, sees only the music. *Howards End* is a musical book, and a complex piece of music at that. Certain key phrases recur, like *Leitmotivs*, the two most prominent being 'Panic and emptiness' and 'telegrams and anger', each of them coined by a Schlegel sister. The fact that these phrases keep appearing insures that the progress of the novel takes place within a kind of Schlegel consciousness. Intimacy, once more, is the prevailing tone.

'Panic and emptiness' is first coined by Helen at the concert: it expresses her feelings, as in the scherzo, when she thinks of 'the goblins' stalking across the world.

They were not aggressive creatures; it was that that made them so terrible to Helen. They merely observed in passing that there was no such thing as splendour or heroism in the world. . . . Helen could not contradict them, for, once at all events, she had felt the same, and had seen the reliable walls of youth collapse. Panic and emptiness! Panic and emptiness! The goblins were right.

The phrase directs us to the results of spiritual muddledom, of denying the priorities of individuality in the name of second-hand experience: confronted with reality the inward self breaks down. But there is a further twist, for the panic and emptiness is not only to be felt: it is to be inflicted. Without the words being used, we sense their presence in the scene towards the end where Henry and Margaret are approaching Howards End in secret, with a doctor, in order to trap Helen before she returns abroad to have her baby.

The doctor, a very young man, began to ask questions about Helen. Was she normal? Was there anything congenital or hereditary? Had anything occurred that was likely to alienate her from her family?

'Nothing,' answered Margaret, wondering what would have happened if she had added: 'Though she did resent my husband's immorality.'

'She always was highly strung,' pursued Henry leaning back in the car as it shot past the church. 'A tendency to spiritualism and those things, though nothing serious. Musical, literary, artistic, but I should say normal – a very charming girl.'

Margaret's anger and terror increased every moment. How dare these men label her sister! What horrors lay ahead! What impertinences that shelter under the name of science! The pack was turning on Helen, to deny her human rights, and it seemed to Margaret that all Schlegels were threatened with her.   (Ch. 35)

This passage has a prophetic ring; none the less Helen has brought this situation upon herself. However strong the indictment of the heartless moral standards of the Wilcox world, by neglecting the good in that world she has laid herself open to panic and emptiness at its hands.

It is Margaret who coins the expression 'telegrams and anger', to cover the kind of nonsensical fuss attendant on Helen and Paul's momentary love affair. Because the Wilcox world omits to take seriously the personal values upheld by the Schlegels, it is helpless in an emotional crisis. (Though it is worth pointing out that in this instance all the fuss, Aunt Juley's interference included, is generated by the Schlegels.) Both parties need each other; or so Margaret, and presumably her creator, believes. But

Forster is too intelligent a novelist to attempt any cut-and-dried balance of forces.

Another recurring theme is that of houses, the character of the places where people make their homes. Forster does not have the brilliant power of, say, Elizabeth Bowen to evoke the atmosphere of domestic interiors, but his gifts in that direction are not inconsiderable. Howards End itself is understandably vivid; but Oniton, the country house in Shropshire, and Leonard's wretched little sitting room are portrayed with equal skill. The importance of living in the right house is something that brings Margaret and Henry together, and it is one of the first things that he discusses with her after their engagement. It does in one way determine the action of the book. Forster remarks of the coming demolition of the block of flats in Wickham Place where the sisters live that we are moving into the civilisation of luggage; and the transience and mobility of people's dwellings is as much a feature of this novel as it is of *Jude the Obscure*. It is for this reason that, much as Margaret likes it, Oniton will never be her home.

But Wickham Place, her home until her marriage, is doomed: the new block of flats which is to take its place is but one among many such buildings, which are seen here as a product of the Wilcox spirit. Perhaps the finest example in the novel of this aspect of old England threatened is when Margaret pays a visit to Howards End to inspect her furniture and finds it all unpacked by Miss Avery. The village with its Hertfordshire charm, the pleasantness of her walk tempered by the depressing gentility of Miss Avery's urbanised niece prepare us for the dramatic *fait accompli* of the newly furnished house. It is a beautiful piece of narrative, realistic and yet filled with an oblique poetic quality that is highly characteristic of its author. Forster seldom overstates his effects (when he does, as in the invocation to England above Poole Harbour, the results are embarrassing). His natural method is indirection, an inferential manner of narration; and the use of coincidence – as in the embankment scene, where Mr Wilcox comes across the two sisters and gives them the fatal advice that Leonard should leave his job – tends as it does in *Jude the Obscure*, to emphasise the disconnectedness of modern life, which is a leading motif in the novel. If the book gives a lean and cerebral impression at times, that too is in keeping with its subject matter.

Another symbol of mobility and uprootedness is the motor car. It recurs throughout the book, beginning on a note of high comedy with Charles and Aunt Juley's disastrous ride back to Howards End (perhaps the funniest scene Forster ever wrote), continuing with the drive to Oniton, when Margaret so satisfactorily jumps out after they have run over a cat, and ending on a sinister note with the episode quoted above, when Margaret and Mr Wilcox go in quest of Helen at Howards End. The big car takes on the characteristics of a hearse. Cars, proprieties – and servants: Aunt Juley may have what her creator calls *'esprit de classe'*, but Margaret sees the whole social structure as fundamentally irresponsible. 'Ladies sheltering behind men, men sheltering behind servants – the whole system's wrong, and she must challenge it.' Again and again it is demonstrated that the Wilcox way of life, based on the priority of money and possessions, is dependent on a social structure that in all vital respects holds it captive.

Margaret is both its challenger and the one who attempts to see it at its best, recognising that it is necessary to her. The attempt to wed the two worlds of 'the prose and the passion' is acted out in her own marriage. But that cannot be said to be a success: Margaret fails in her attempt to make Henry see his inconsistency over his own conduct with Jacky and that of Helen. But none the less her speech is memorable:

Not any more of this! . . . You shall see the connection if it kills you, Henry! You have had a mistress – I forgave you. My sister has a lover – you drive her from the house. Do you see the connection? Stupid, hypocritical, cruel – oh, contemptible! – a man who insults his wife when she's alive and cants with her memory when she's dead. A man who ruins a woman for his pleasure, and casts her off to ruin other men. And gives bad financial advice, and then says he is not responsible. These men are you. You can't recognize them, because you cannot connect. I've had enough of your unweeded kindness. I've spoilt you long enough. All your life you've been spoiled. Mrs Wilcox spoiled you. No one has ever told you what you are – muddled, criminally muddled. Men like you use repentance as a blind, so don't repent. Only say to yourself, 'What Helen has done, I've done.'   (Ch. 38)

Margaret's plain speaking is heard still more unforgettably in an earlier scene with Aunt Juley (surely the most endearing of Forster's various geese?). It is, incidentally, a good example of the way in which he laces his more serious moments with comedy, a kind of sugaring the pill, if pill it be. His words are well worn now, but at the time they chimed in with much *avant-garde* writing, and reveal Margaret as, presumably, an admirer of George Bernard Shaw.

'I hope to risk things all my life.'

'Oh, Margaret, most dangerous.'

'But after all,' she continued with a smile, 'there's never any great risk as long as you have money.'

'Oh, shame! What a shocking speech!'

'Money pads the edges of things,' said Miss Schlegel, 'God help those who have none.'

'But this is something quite new!' said Mrs Munt, who collected new ideas as a squirrel collects nuts, and was especially attracted by those that are portable.

'New for me: sensible people have acknowledged it for years. You and I and the Wilcoxes stand upon money as upon islands. It is so firm beneath our feet that we forget its very existence. It's only when we see someone near us tottering that we realize all that an independent income means. Last night . . . I began to think that the lowest abyss is not the absence of love, but the absence of coin.'   (Ch. 7)

Margaret is not, of course, to endorse this entirely (note the subtly distancing effect of that 'Miss Schlegel': Miss Schlegel is holding forth a little). But her point of view is a necessary check to the kind of idealism that governs her life and Helen's. And it is to Helen that this speech is really directed, rather than to Mrs Munt. (The latter thinks it's 'more like Socialism'.)

If Margaret is in some danger of seeming a prig, she is saved from this not only by the actual outcome of events, and the tragic realisation of her mistakes, but by lesser touches, such as the way we see her through other people's eyes – Leonard's, for instance ('the toothy one'), or those of Charles and Dolly. She is put in the wrong by Mrs Wilcox, whose letter in reply to Margaret's declining further acquaintance is crushing in its simplicity. She behaves impulsively, foolishly, and she can mount the soap-box. We are all too aware of her lack of physical charm. But she is honest, and true of heart: more than any other Forster character she provides us with a trustworthy moral centre for the book. Moreover, as Rose Macaulay observes, she has

> most of the attributes that please civilized women in one another. Beauty, merely feminine charm, single-track emotion, biological urge – these qualities, so confusing and swamping to personality and character, so much the stock-in-trade of the heroine-maker in [her] scarcely exist.[11]

It is, and is intended to be, high praise.

But one thing that neither Margaret nor her creator can do is to persuade us of the admirable qualities of Henry Wilcox. They may be stated, but they are never shown. We may admire Margaret's capacity for love, but not the cause of it. Henry is too like the pompous male manager who has to be satirised, and portrayed partly as an overgrown child, in the work of many women novelists – 'Elizabeth' notably, but also E. H. Young, Nancy Mitford, E. M. Delafield: the list is long. Forster's failure here is an example of the femininity (as distinct from femaleness) of his sensitivity; and is the price he pays for his success with the character of Margaret Schlegel.

Indeed, if Margaret can attract she can also annoy: this, one suspects, being a necessary aspect of the book. For *Howards End*, for all its urbanity, its crowd of entertaining characters – Aunt Juley, Tibby, Dolly Wilcox and the rest – is designed less to amuse than to disturb. Forster achieves this not by any frontal attack on the reader's conscience or any rhetorical declamation on the condition of England, but by telling us a tale of a group of unremarkable people who, amid all the apparently directionless changes and chances of life, are buffeted together and, because of the confusion in their moral outlooks, do each other tremendous harm. The very jerkiness of the narration, the authorial intrusions, the stabs of angry irony and sharply lyrical beauty, the coincidences and disproportionate accounts of events and happenings, all go to make a novel that feels as full of light and shade as the changing society it was seeking to portray. For all its many shortcomings *Howards End* remains a permanently readable book; and, if lacking the artistic perfection of Forster's first and last novels, it nevertheless retains its hold on the imagination by obeying, however fitfully, its heroine's injunction to unite the passion with the prose. In Laurence Brander's words, 'The novel is part of the evolving social consciousness of the English people.'[12]

III

The high esteem, not to say veneration, in which Forster was held in the last two decades of his life has not made it easy to appreciate the achievement of his early novels. The social commentator, the spokesman who became a kind of intellectual's J. B. Priestley, throws back a light on his career that colours it with the mellow glow supposed to emanate from sages. The resident pride of King's, the quietly impressive witness at the Chatterley trial, was also known as a classic author, his name linked with those of Conrad, Lawrence, Joyce and Virginia Woolf as one of the five prescribed novelists for any orthodox course on twentieth-century fiction. And yet, placed beside those names, his own resounds less forcibly with associations. One novel, *A Passage to India*, is unquestionably a major achievement; but the rest of Forster's output, lacking Conrad's sonorous profundities, the angry energy of Lawrence, the verbal inventiveness and dedicated artistry of Woolf and Joyce, can seem trivial and even half-hearted. His name does not lend itself easily to homage.

Not that he would have minded that: the modesty which could irritate his detractors did not exceed its proper depth.

I have no mystic faith in the people. I have in the individual. He seems to me a divine achievement and I mistrust any view which belittles him. If anyone calls you a wretched little individual – and I've been called that – don't you take it lying down.[13]

This was the man of 1946 speaking; but the sharpness had been there from the start. Indeed, the very schoolboyish tone of the last injunction would suggest it. We find it in all those tales about the downtrodden and repressed, from 'The Story of a Panic' onwards. Much of Forster's work constitutes a response rather than a deliberation. When the deliberations come it is as a result of previously followed and understood reactions. The clarity of utterance and insight in his later years was the result of attention to his own experience. And that response was exercised and elicited through the practice of fiction. It is because Forster was such a good novelist that we can accept him as a sage.

The early novels, then, are most properly seen as testing grounds, the delicate exploration of moods and tendencies. If we approach them as a series of considered themes or statements we shall be disappointed: they will seem light, confused, pretentious. Occasionally they are all these things; but their real character is one that compels us to read in such a way that our own responses inevitably declare themselves. We are not so much being told the story as being shown it. And this, Conrad and James apart, the other Edwardian novelists do not do.

Forster's imaginative world is remarkably consistent. It is full of recurring episodes and inner symbols among which he reconnoitres. Paradise regained, or re-attained, is one of them: Italy, Wiltshire, Oniton, Howards End – in each case betrayal, 'crass casualty' and death lurk in them. The place of heart's desire is more dangerous than contemporary Edwardian sentiment would usually allow. The novels are also, in their muted way, tales of a quest; but the hero–heroine proves unworthy of it, even though, where the women are concerned, a last-minute reprieve is granted. (In the case of Lucy Honeychurch this involved Forster in a complete rewriting: the odds against clarity of vision are heavy.) And everywhere the enemy, like the 'they' of Edward Lear's limericks, are at hand to smash the nonconformist; but in Forster's world they end, when at their most brutal, as victims of the very violence they have invoked: Charles Wilcox and Gerald Dawes are the most spectacular instances of this. (It is a suggestive coincidence in this connexion that Lawrence was to use both the name Dawes and the name Gerald for two of his own more violent characters, in *Sons and Lovers* and *Women in Love* respectively.) Alternatively the enemy can be outwitted by the innocents, of whom Stephen Wonham is an obvious example. Thus the lines of hero–villain and good–evil are blurred: there is no inner logic in events any more than there is external justice. Forster portrays a world ruled by chance. The emancipation from nineteenth-century literary determinism is complete. It is this, perhaps, more than anything else which has kept these novels acceptable to a later generation when the more formally 'modern' novels of the time have dated.

This relativity extends to our notions of time and meaning. Births, deaths, marriages are mentioned perfunctorily: clock time is secondary to the measurement of time by value. There are curious foreshortenings of action, brief fights that seem to be parodies of genuine aggression. Arrivals by train are slow, and observed as if in a picture show, like that of Margaret from the downs above Swanage after she has accepted Henry Wilcox; or they are botched (invariably, we may be sure) like Cousin Charlotte's. A murder takes place almost unnoticed, someone jumps out of a moving motor car, a bookcase collapses, a carriage overturns: the novels' pace is odd and jerky, and nothing seems to happen gradually. Forster's world is the very reverse of that of Bennett in *The Old Wives' Tale*. Planned enjoyments prove fatal to peace: one thinks of the Herritons' disastrous rescue operation, the expedition on which Rickie denies his brother, the picnic where Cousin Charlotte watches Lucy being kissed, Evie's wedding, and that other, more fatal picnic which ended in a panic – not for nothing does Aunt Juley (always so wrong) determine on her (needless to say supposititious) deathbed that Helen and Margaret shall take the Lulworth trip. A sense of unease is induced by these methods: the massive fabric of society is seen to be made up of individuals, all of whom are the sport of chance.

The contrast between the individual and the corporate is nowhere more tellingly made than in the treatment of women. If individual women are presented sympathetically, there is over and above them a kind of impersonal witch, a Forsterian embodiment of 'the mothers', known in current social terms as 'ladies', whose function it would seem to be to disrupt male pleasure and peace, and to be the ruination of common sense. She is invoked in all the novels, comically in *A Room with a View,* resignedly in *The Longest Journey*, bitterly in *Maurice*, and with deadly seriousness as the concept reaches its logical fulfilment in *A Passage to India*. The male villain is one who trades on, and helps to create, the 'ladies' chimera. At his most crass, like Charles Wilcox, he refers to 'the women', but at his most deadly he discards them altogether. More generally present are those fatuous males who delight in the admiration of women, while at the same time submitting them to an insufferable patronage.

Forster seems to be trying to reach the essential feminine virtues by mocking, or by criticising, the male attempt to evade them through subduing them to artificial conventions. Although it is possible to detect an anti-female bias in his work, it is really in the interests of feminine values and fulfilment that he writes, and the kind of wisdom he advocates goes well beyond the contemporary sexual polarisations. Even as a homosexual he was ahead of his time.

9 *Maurice* and the Later Stories

I

The friendship between Forster and D. H. Lawrence contains an element of comedy. Following his near-disastrous visit to the Sussex cottage where the Lawrences were staying in 1915, a visit in which he was subjected to his full share of Lawrentian eloquence, both male and female, Forster was described by his host to Bertrand Russell in terms that have, in the light of our subsequent knowledge, a certain cruel irony.

> Forster . . . is bound hand and foot bodily. Why? *Because he does not believe that any beauty or any divine utterance is any good any more. . . .* But why can't he act? Why can't he take a woman and fight clear to his own basic, primal being? Because he knows that self-realization is not his ultimate desire. His ultimate desire is for the renewed action which has been called the social passion – the love for humanity – the desire to work for humanity.[1]

There is so much insight in this, it is so near the point of Forster's work while in fact missing it, that it provides a perfect example of that failure to connect which was one of Forster's own obsessions. Lawrence, like so many people, was both attracted by Forster's honesty and straight thinking, and repelled by the cautious, self-derogatory style in which he chose to present himself. And this view of him as a buttoned-up, repressed and milk-and-water liberal has been strengthened in some quarters by the posthumous revelation that he was homosexual. It has indeed on occasion been amusing to watch the tightrope act performed by critics whose anxiety to exercise the required tolerance has been bedevilled by their own instinctive treatment

129

of Forster as somehow sick, or debarred from writing in a fully mature manner, because, to quote Samuel Hynes, 'of a suppressed guilty sexuality'. The same critic confidently goes on to state that 'Most obviously, Forster could not imagine any aspect of the range of experience between men and women – heterosexual attraction, heterosexual relations, marriage were mysterious to him.'[2]

But 'any aspect' is here limited to a sexual meaning. There are other relations possible between men and women, and Forster writes of them with obvious familiarity. However, he does show a sympathy with the emotionally ill constituted that is alien to our robuster sexual orthodoxies; and, as H. J. Oliver points out, 'of the sexless type, and of the older woman, he shows an exceptional understanding'.[3] Only John Cowper Powys and Ivy Compton-Burnett (strangely assorted pair) can match him in that particular combination.

Hynes is more to the point when he stresses the importance of Forster's sexual nature as characterising (as distinct from limiting) his imagination. But to identify that nature with 'the voyeuristic distancing of the narration, the ironic tone, the self-deprecating humour' is again to oversimplify. And it leaves out of account the basic consideration in any treatment of a homosexual writer: his necessary, imposed estrangement from society, his sense of inner rejection and hurt in the face of what is at best a patronising acceptance of his condition, and at worst a scornful or vindictive rejection of it. If Forster is a major homosexual novelist it is because he put that estrangement and hurt to positive use, and, to quote Hynes approvingly this time, 'made out of self-deprecation, transference, and evasion, a personal and functioning style'.[4] The transformation of a private and personal estrangement into an engaged concern with the very society which implicitly rejected him is one of Forster's triumphs as humanist and artist. And he effects this not by political attack or ethical polemic, but by tracing the process through which men and women move from self-imprisonment to joy.

For one theme that is central in all four of Forster's early novels is that of conversion: the change in outlook caused by a moment of spiritual illumination. The concept is, fundamentally, a religious one, for it presupposes a moral absolute governing the individual's sense of direction – the latter word being taken in its meaning of 'being directed' as well as in that of destination. 'What happens next' matters because of the relation between the events of the story and their consequence in the minds of the characters. But religion as such meant little to Forster; the claims of 'poor talkative little Christianity',[5] as he called it, were secondary to a sense of the significant, of our imagination's power to respond to, and to make sense of, the events in which we find ourselves involved. The conversions in his fiction may be towards the fulfilment of a moral ideal, a movement from darkness to light; but even more important is the movement from sorrow to joy. The characters are feeling their way out of a condition of frustration and misery into one of freedom and a capacity for happiness. They do not, Lucy apart, do more than gesture towards these ends; but they are aware of them. If in *Howards End* Margaret seems over-aware of the limitations of others, Helen experiences a baptismal experience into fulfilment without any conscious repentance. In that novel the moral strands are curiously twisted; and it may be yet another reason for Forster's dissatisfaction with it. In *Maurice*, however, the issues are spelled out plain.

For the conversion from misery to joy is the goal of that need for personal awakening which the homosexual Forster was, in the conditions under which he lived, bound to experience in himself. Just as in his fiction he was prohibited from speaking out (Arnold's critique of Gray comes readily to mind here, for Gray too was a man who suffered agonies from emotional suppression) so in his own life Forster found it impossible to be what he was. But the need for disguise can poison creativity at its source, and the writing of an explicitly homosexual novel became an act of imaginative therapy. Imaginative rather than moral: Forster does not appear to have suffered those feelings of conscious guilt about his nature which are frequently supposed (not to say required) to be attendant on it. (That *Maurice* is the product of what George Steiner in a perceptive and sympathetic essay has called 'an intensely spiritualized yet nervous and partly embittered sexuality'[6] at the *unconscious* level is a different matter.) Moreover, Forster's determination that his book should have a happy ending may be seen not as compensatory fantasy but as a demonstration that homosexual love, which is usually regarded merely as a problem to be analysed and overhauled by social worker, psychologist and priest, can be to those experiencing it a matter of normality and joy. *Maurice* was not a coming to terms with something ugly or rejected; rather it was in the nature of a stolen holiday by which Forster hoped that his frustrated muse might profit. The very fact that it was not written for publication gives it an interest apart from its actual theme. For, the 'official' readership being removed, we are in the position of seeing what Forster was prepared to say to himself, and that on a subject which had been the driving force behind the earlier novels. It was an examination of the very springs of his creativity.

Maurice, however, offers peculiar difficulties to the critic. As John Colmer rightly observes,

> The absence of a bracing tension between the author and a wider public accounts for the unworked thinness of much of the narrative, its self-indulgent tone, the too intermittent play of irony. Clearly one of the worst evils of literary censorship is that it drives the writer in on himself, with a consequent impoverishment in moral vision.[7]

Appearing privately, and written ahead of its time, *Maurice* can only be compared with its author's previous writings; while being neither pornography nor eroticism, it does not belong to the category of subterranean novels. Its aim was to provide an education in feeling.

Although it is not easy, today, to appreciate the emotional reticence with which the book was written, it should not be too difficult to understand the stress. As Forster wrote in the terminal note of 1960, since 1913 'there has been a change in the public attitude here: the change from ignorance and terror to familiarity and contempt'. The latter response can be no less harmful than the former, harmful to the holders of it as much as to the victims; and it certainly revealed itself in some reviews when the book was published. John Saye Martin's claim that 'In today's world Maurice could have been an active and happy homosexual as well as a stockbroker'[8] is surely over-optimistic.

II

The problem for the homosexual novelist (as distinct from the novelist writing about homosexuals) is to preserve the particular quality of his sensibility without being forced into special pleading by society's attitude, and thus into playing the enemy's game. For, while not belonging to a universally outlawed state, he is bound, because of social ostracism, to regard 'the world' as being an enemy; and yet for that very reason he is well qualified to write a certain kind of social protest novel. It is in this light that *Maurice* may be most profitably approached.

To speak of a distinctively homosexual sensibility, however, is to oversimplify: better to think in terms of an infinite variety of sexual shadings in an infinite variety of human beings. In Forster's particular case we find a sensibility that is aroused by the notion of the masculine as such, and by the male in love, and most especially by the man who can be tender to his fellow male: the various Italians are cases in point, as are George Emerson and Stephen Wonham. In each case Forster identifies himself with the woman concerned or, as with Philip Herriton and Rickie Elliot, with a man who is given womanly characteristics: there is in this way a highlighting of the masculine. Similar effects can be seen in Lawrence's novels and in those of John Cowper Powys; but Forster lacks the capacity of these two writers to transfer themselves from sex to sex, and thus to make their women as powerful sexual agents as their men. Sexually speaking, Forster's women are, it must be conceded, a lifeless lot.

In *Maurice*, however, perhaps because the sexual question is confronted directly, we have an interesting shift in tone. Until Alec Scudder appears on the scene, the erotic element is all but non-existent – the young man Dicky being the blatant, exactly timed exception. What we are left with is a harsh, unremitting account of what the exclusions of sexual orthodoxy inflict upon the involuntary dissenter. The emphasis is on social nonconformity as much as on individual consciousness.

Indeed, as a novel of homosexual love, *Maurice* must be accounted a partial failure, memorable though much of it is. Its story, for one of Forster's, is straightforward. Maurice Hall lives with, and is dominated by, his mother and two younger sisters. While at Cambridge he meets and falls in love with a fellow undergraduate called Clive Durham. Clive returns his feelings, but by mutual though confused agreement the affair remains Platonic. In due course Clive gets married, and Maurice is forced to realise the true nature of his feelings and desires; but having sentimentalised them, he readily falls in with society's verdict that he is 'an unspeakable of the Oscar Wilde sort'. Attempts to cure himself come to nothing, and he withers slowly in the hostile air of contemporary morality. Then, while on a visit to Clive and his wife Anne at their country house in Wiltshire (but sited on the borders of leafy, magical, legend-haunted Somerset), he encounters Alec Scudder, a gamekeeper on the estate, and spends the night with him. When Alec seeks to renew contact, Maurice, class-ridden, suspects him of attempted blackmail; but, after Alec has proved his sincerity by refusing at the last moment to emigrate to the Argentine, the two men decide to throw in their lot together. Maurice gives up his job, and they depart for 'the greenwood', where, Lytton Strachey was to comment, 'I should have prophesied a rupture after six months'. But Forster was unrepentant about his happy ending. It met a personal need, even if it tended to blunt his message.

Far more damaging is Forster's uncertainty in handling the love scenes; his language is perfervid, the physicalities inhibited, and the whole effect, as Steiner says, is one of 'defensive pathos'.[9] The crucial figure here is Clive. That his personality is subtly portrayed is not in this instance quite enough: his physical presence is needed if we are to share Maurice's tension and frustration to the full. But that presence is lacking: the early scenes between the two young men have a softness that is no substitute for eroticism, and the effect is now embarrassing. Indeed, Clive's determination to keep the affair Platonic, while consistent with the emotional sublimations of the time, does as it stands weaken the contrast between him and Alec. They are too different for it to be felt. Maurice's compliance, while understandable, is weak: the relationship disguises his true nature instead of revealing it. And yet the author appears to endorse it for more than it proves to be worth. Clive's decision to get married ('Against my will I have become normal. I cannot help it' – the implausibility of that statement is something that Forster never really dissects) – while abrupt, is not for that reason unconvincing: it merely lies outside the scope of the book. But, by avoiding the physical implications of Clive's relationship with Maurice, Forster makes it impossible for us to be interested in his relationship with Anne. What we know of it is chilling.

Nevertheless, to talk at all in these terms while discussing a Forster novel is to indicate where the importance of *Maurice* lies:

this book is exploring the physical roots of his imaginative world. And here Clive is rejected as firmly and ruthlessly as Cecil Vyse and Henry Wilcox are rejected. He is muddled, and for all his idealism and fine country house (which, significantly, is in a state of slow decay) he belongs to the world of Sawston. The denial of the flesh is a denial of the spirit also. Forster never wrote more scathingly than in those passages when Clive, after his marriage, patronises Maurice for his failure to follow suit. Maurice is going to London to consult a hypnotist, and allows Clive to believe that it is to seek a wife.

'I've thought more often of you than you imagine, Maurice my dear. As I said last autumn, I care for you in the real sense, and always shall. We were young idiots, weren't we? – but one can get something even out of idiocy. Development. No, more than that, intimacy. You and I know and trust one another just because we were once idiots. Marriage has made no difference. Oh, that's jolly, I do think –'

'You give me your blessing then?'

'I should think so!'

'Thanks.'

Clive's eyes softened. He wanted to convey something warmer than development. Dare he borrow a gesture from the past?

'Think of me all tomorrow,' said Maurice, 'and as for Anne – she may think of me too.'

So gracious a reference decided him to kiss the fellow very gently on his big brown hand.

Maurice shuddered.

'You don't mind?'

'Oh, no.'

'Maurice dear, I wanted just to show I hadn't forgotten the past. I quite agree – don't let's mention it ever again, but I wanted to show just this once.'

'All right.'

'Aren't you thankful it's ended properly?'

'How properly?'

'Instead of that muddle last year.'

'Oh with you.'

'Quits, and I'll go.'

Maurice applied his lips to the starched cuff of a dress shirt.

Having functioned, he withdrew, leaving Clive more friendly
than ever, and insistent he should return to Penge as soon as
circumstances allowed this.   (Ch. 35)

The restraint of this is not, perhaps, to contemporary taste; but
the tension, pain, irony and anger behind the dialogue are
unmistakable. Much is gathered from those verbs – 'convey',
'borrow', 'decided', 'applied', 'functioned'. The indictment is
implacable; and the sense of Maurice's baffled misery and
despair is exactly caught in a dialogue that leaves much to the
reader's own perceptions. Forster's gift for understatement
serves him well here. And that starched cuff is recalled unforgettably at the end of the novel when Clive, having heard
about Alec and responded with shock and disbelief, is told by
Maurice, 'you don't love me. I was yours once till death if you'd
cared to keep me, but I'm someone else's now – I can't hang
about whining for ever – and he's mine in a way that shocks you,
but why don't you stop being shocked, and attend to your own
happiness?' (Ch. 46). That speech has a vigour in marked
contrast with the ironies and playfulness in the earlier novels;
but Clive's final refusal to come to terms with the truth is in
keeping with an exacting moral vision that had attended the
author's work from the start. He refuses to take Maurice seriously, and holds him to a dinner appointment. 'His last words were
"Next Wednesday, say at 7.45. Dinner-jacket's enough, as you
know."'

The early days at Cambridge are described with a truthfulness
that makes its own point: the adolescent nature of the relationship is plain. The use of Maurice's motor-cycle and side-car as
an agent of the young men's deliverance from decanal authority
and social pressures reverses previous associations with motor
cars: significantly, however, the machine breaks down, and is
left in a ditch in the fens. Today the emphasis on innocent
idealism is less familiar than is the inbuilt inhibition that makes
Maurice answer a shout through his window while Clive is
sitting on his knee. The dominance and intrusion of the conventional outer world is painfully conveyed here and in other places
in the novel, and underlines Forster's insistence on the sacredness of private life.

Maurice's response when he is called is offset by his own call,
'Come!' after the desolating scene with Clive, quoted earlier. The

subsequent repeated cry, followed by Alec's entry through the window, is appropriate enough, if a shade implausible: the trouble is that, though Forster's myth-making imagination serves him well here, his failure, voluntary or otherwise, to actualise the love encounter between the two men leaves him with a situation which can easily be branded as sentimental. It is too romantic, too genteel even, and the episode seems conceived in terms less appropriate to Alec than to Clive, whose beliefs it is intended to refute. What is interesting about Maurice's affair with Alec is Forster's handling of a theme which had always interested him – that of class. One reward of the homosexual condition is that it readily transcends class barriers; and in the chapter where Maurice and Alec confront each other in the British Musem, one of the strongest that Forster ever wrote, the struggle in them both between their sense of class and their belief in their own humanity is riveting. And Alec's letter rebuking Maurice gives one the same feeling of salutary discomfort as does Mrs Wilcox's rebuke to Margaret Schlegel. It is Forster's most testing confrontation with the claims of love, and Lytton Strachey's comment, though reasonable enough when out of context, is not quite on the target.

In order to reach the greenwood where he can be free to love another human being in the way his nature dictates, Maurice confronts the men in authority, whom, as I. A. Richards once pointed out,[10] Forster always treates unfairly – for reasons now more clear than at the time (1927) when the criticism was made. He has to pass the four guardians of society – the schoolmaster, the doctor, the scientist and the priest. All four in their different ways condemn him, and not one of them can offer any help. The schoolmaster is ineffective, though the novel's opening scene when Maurice receives his sex instruction by means of drawings upon the sand (which the master forgets to wipe out) is extremely funny. The doctor, on the other hand, proves ignorant and fatuous; more humane than the 'scientific' hypnotist, he is yet incapable of understanding, or of feeling for, any departure from what he regards as the norm. The hypnotist, when he finds that he cannot effect a 'cure', is simply bored: thus Forster comments on the impersonality of scientific method when applied to human beings, and demonstrates the impossibility of there being any help, other than love, for one who wandered, 'the wrong words on his lips and the wrong desires in his heart, and his arms full of air'. Certainly none is forthcoming from the priest. Mr Borenius is far more unnerving than the usual ineffective run of Forsterian clergymen. The portrait is sparsely drawn, but, as with Mr Beebe, we are made aware of a disdain of the sexual act as such which breeds an instinct for its possible frustration. The scene at the close of the book when he talks with Maurice at Southampton is the last and most testing of the latter's trials. He is saved from despair at the priest's intolerance less by his own courage than by the realisation of how Alec has defied it.

'Mr Borenius assumed that love between two men must be ignoble, and so could not interpret what had happened.' But Maurice, who has found that such love has ennobled him and Alec, can interpret without difficulty.

> He had brought out the man in Alec, and now it was Alec's turn to bring out the hero in him. He knew what the call was, and what his answer must be. They must live outside class, without relations or money; they must work and stick to each other till death.   (Ch. 45)

There is a sense of pilgrimage about Maurice's journey; and Alec's determination stands in marked contrast with the dithering of one who lives in 'a land of facilities'.

Maurice's dreams are symptomatic. One of them is with 'a nondescript' with whom he is playing football. He turns out to be the gardener's boy with whom Maurice has played as a child ('Ansell' in the story of that name). He is naked, another version of the demon boy; but when Maurice is about to grapple with him he wakes up with 'a brutal disappointment'. The boy is both resented and desired. The other dream is more idealised, and thus more acceptable: 'He scarcely saw a face, scarcely heard a voice say, "That is your friend," and then it was over, having filled him with beauty, and taught him tenderness' (Ch. 3).

The separation of the two dreams constitutes a separation between soul and body which issues in alternate brutality and slush, such as Maurice's sisters show to him after his rustication. The second dream, taken alone, is insidiously dangerous. It bears some affinities with one recorded by Forster's friend Forrest Reid, whose romantic novels about boyhood he greatly liked. In Reid's dream the two figures are united.

I was waiting for someone who had never failed me – my friend in this place, who was infinitely dearer to me than any friend I had on earth. And presently, out from the leafy shadow he bounded into the sunlight. I saw him standing for a moment, his naked body the colour of pale amber against the dark background – a boy of about my own age, with eager parted lips and bright eyes. But he was more beautiful than anything else in the whole world, or in my imagination.[11]

The very lack of tension in Reid's account may argue a more fortunate lot than Forster's (indeed, the strange and effective conclusion of his autobiography, *Apostate,* from which this account comes, suggests it). But 'perfection of the life or of the work' – Yeats's dictum applies to Reid and Forster; and if Forster himself, like Maurice, suffered a divided consciousness, his art was to profit by it.

It is notable that Alec Scudder is very different from the idealised figure of Reid's dream. He combines roughness with tenderness, male with female, in a manner reminiscent of Stephen Wonham. But Alec is quite without Stephen's immaturity or playfulness. He offers an adult relationship and an adult confrontation with the world. He is a strangely autonomous being for Forster to create, and seems to have stepped into the world of his creator's novels very much as he climbed through Maurice's window.

But that world is not noticeably evident in *Maurice,* which helps to account for the disappointment with which it was greeted on publication. The family ambience so engagingly presented in *A Room with a View* is here portrayed as sterile; there is no whimsy or ironic play, beyond such mild and characteristic comedy as we find in the scene when the undergraduate Maurice tells his mother about his atheism.

'I knew you would be upset. I cannot help it, mother dearest. I am made that way and it is no good arguing.'
    'Your poor father always went to church.'
    'I'm not my father.'
    'Morrie, Morrie, what a thing to say.'
    'Well, he isn't' said Kitty in her perky way. 'Really, mother, come.'
    'Kitty, dear, you here,' cried Mrs Hall, feeling that disap-

proval was due and unwilling to bestow it on her son. 'We were talking about things not suited, and you are perfectly wrong besides, for Maurice is the image of his father – Dr Barry said so.'

'Well, Dr Barry doesn't go to church himself,' said Maurice, falling into the family habit of talking all over the shop.   (Ch. 8)

Out of context this reads like gentle fun; but in the face of Maurice's alienated state such inconsequence is ominous.

Such further humour as there is is tart; the novel's strength is felt less in its inventiveness than in its anger, its careful craftsmanship, and the way in which it makes the homosexual's predicament symbolic of any outlawed condition within an intolerant society. Forster's most tenacious indictment of that spiritual materialism which marked his age (and which continues, under new guises, to mark our own), *Maurice* lacks the participatory understanding to be found in the earlier novels. In this respect, as in most others, it is inferior to them, nor is it likely to be a general favourite; but in writing it Forster cleared his mind of an emotional block and so achieved the balance, vigour and detachment that went to the creation of the masterpiece that was to follow it a decade later.

III

Even more than *Maurice*, Forster's late stories pose problems for the reader. His own valuation of them was confused. Although written, he said, 'not to express myself but to excite myself' he felt that they were 'a wrong channel for my pen'.[12] He burnt some of these stories in 1922; those that survive were either written later or were saved by the approval of his friends. They demand a certain suspension of accustomed sensitivity from such of his readers as may be inclined with Jeffrey Meyers to dismiss them as 'puerile, pathetic, sentimental and thoroughly unimaginative fantasies'.[13] But, read sympathetically, they are not pornographic, though one or two are decidedly and cheerfully erotic. All are filled with a vigour and intention lacking in the weaker of his earlier tales.

Four of them are light-hearted, not to say ribald, in tone,

written with the desire to outrage Sawston standards. In this they differ markedly from the final tale, 'The Other Boat', which evokes a compassionate indignation, and from *Maurice*. In the latter the Platonic idealism of the world of Carpenter and Lowes Dickinson, which sought to counter the social rejection of homosexuality with a specific and superior Uranian (the term is Carpenter's) morality of its own, leads to an enfeeblement of sensory presentation. The novel was a plea to the world; but the late stories were written *at* the world, and replace apologetic with attack. They make their points through scorn, and that in the name of a wider sensuality than their ostensible occasion.

The hypocrisy, confusion and dangerous (though frequently creative) repressiveness of the late-nineteenth-century sexual ethics under which Forster grew up are supposed to have been left behind today. But the flourishing pornographic-film industry and much contemporary fiction in fact cater for a taste essentially parasitic upon hereditary repressions; while psychological, social, and commercial pressures enforce, almost as much as Victorian religion inhibited, displays of sexual feeling. In each case there is an embargo on tenderness; and both Forster and Lawrence (who invested that word with a depth of meaning peculiar to him) were tilting at the same enemy, though, of the two, it was Lawrence who was to draw out the connection between sexual ethics and the social and economic structures which support them. Forster's sexual nature, however, gave him a viewpoint of his own. The element of play is prominent in these stories; they might have been written with the homosexual's use of 'gay' in mind. They satirise contemporary repressive legislation in the name of uncomplicated sensuality. As Mirko says in 'What Does It Matter?', 'Poking doesn't count.' It is something done by (nearly) everybody.

This particular story is a 'Ruritanian' fantasy, and one of the funniest that Forster ever wrote. The scheming Count Waghagrhen desires to topple the President of Pottibakia, and contrives that its First Lady shall discover him in bed with his mistress. As it turns out, the mistress is far more shocked than is the wife, whose main concern is to get her lunch. He then arranges for the President's seduction by a young guardsman in the mistress's villa, to be followed by their discovery by both ladies (not to mention the Bessarabian ambassador and his wife). But in the end all three decide that there is nothing here to make a fuss about. It is not necessary to pursue the story to its outrageous but salutary conclusion to recognise the author's comment that the social commotion attendant upon sexual irregularity is far more damaging than the irregularity itself: he was to make the same point by implication in *A Passage to India*. Possibly he was recalling the aftermath of that boyhood misadventure on the Downs.

'The Torque', though more irreverent, is less convincing. In the person of the bossy and disagreeable Perpetua, hell-bent on sanctity, the cult of virginity is subject to sharp comment, comment that is more persuasive than are the sexual fantasies of her young brother: in this historical tale Forster seems to have got his literary modes confused, and the writing shows it. Rather more successful is 'The Classical Annex'. This, the slightest of these stories, also draws on the ancient world to make its points: here a large male statue in a provincial museum comes alive with bizarre results. Once again the erotic element is secondary to the exposure of folly. The Councillor who had insisted on the imposition of a fig-leaf is unable to perceive the implications in a statue of two wrestlers. The prude's eye is not innocent but blind.

Forster's aim in these stories is not only to mock the prurient but also to help cast out the prevailing fear that surrounded the subject of sex in contemporary attitudes. Thus in 'The Obelisk' he shows the liberating and not the punishing effects of yielding to casual, friendly desire: a drab middle-aged man and wife are physically renewed by a chance meeting with two sailors. This is a story in which Forster for the one and only time shows an understanding of and sympathy with female sexuality. Another unusual feature of several of these tales (and one in part accounted for by their original purpose) is the spectacle of older men giving and receiving pleasure with younger ones. This is really more unconventional than the homo-erotic content itself, and also serves to reinforce the overall protest against restrictive barriers of sex, class or age.

In 'Arthur Snatchtold', however, such an encounter has a grim outcome. Here the cheerful young milkman who livens up an elderly widowed businessman on a dull weekend is arrested after their encounter, and goes to gaol rather than reveal the identity of his companion – an unlikely event, the cynical may feel. The rather too larky dialogue apart, the story is well told, funny and desolatingly sad. The manoeuvres of the law when trying to interfere with illegal sensuality are exposed as more indecent than the crime itself; while the account of Sir Richard Conway's realisation of his escape perfectly captures the complex emotions of those who run with the hare and hunt with the hounds. What these stories reveal above all is that Forster, when engaged on the theme which inevitably preoccupied him, could write with a power and a directness far removed from the delicate irony with which he is usually associated. The sense of guilt and terror is as pervasive as the note of scornful mockery.

The terror surrounding the legal and social attitudes to homosexual love, the denial that it ever can be honourable love, the association of it with filth, bestiality and other abusive terms reaches its climax in 'Dr Woolacott', 'The Life to Come' and 'The Other Boat'. The first two are fables. In 'Dr Woolacott' the self-punishment theme reappears, as the young invalid squire encounters a phantom labourer who declares that his state is being worsened not cured by the venerated, endlessly solicitous Dr Woolacott. The sick man's dilemma is solved by a death in ecstasy: an ambiguous conclusion. The figure of the doctor is a subtle representation of that view of sex which regards it as something to be considered gingerly or to be treated as a disease. More than once in these tales Forster suggests that, just as it is the attitude of society towards homosexuals which creates most of the problems it deplores, so a repressive attitude to all sexuality can only be met by a refusal to take that repression at its own valuation. '. . . not a single man he touched ever got well. Woolacott dosed, Woolacott inoculated, Woolacott operated, Woolacott spoke a kind word even, and there they were and here they are.'

This case is argued with still greater force in 'The Life to Come'. A beautifully constructed four-act drama, it moves from farce of a mildly salacious kind through satire to stark tragedy. The native chieftain takes quite literally the missionary's call to love, and, by a neat Forsterian irony, wholesale conversion follows on a night of illegal and, from the missionary's point of view, immoral sexual congress. The remorseful Mr Pinmay is unable to clear up the misunderstanding, and rewards the long years of Vithobai's patient wooing with rejection. His murder by

Vithobai (now renamed Barnabas) on the latter's deathbed forms a logical conclusion: if love has divided them, then death shall not. This tale shows the poetic nature of Forster's imagination. The story works through its symbols – the hut where they 'share', the wood where the missionary refuses to follow, the death-in-life endured by Vithobai followed by the life-in-death posited for Pinmay. The contrast between the rigid European Christian code and the more relaxed ethic of the native resembles that made in 'The Torque' (though in fact 'primitive' man is less easy in his sexual behaviour than modern Western man would like to think). The names too – Pinmay, Barnabas (which means 'Son of Consolation') – have dramatic force. The latter's speech speaks for more than his immediate situation: 'First the grapes of my body are pressed. Then I am silenced. Now I am punished. Night, evening and a day. What remains?' The cadence and vocabulary of this are reminiscent of T. F. Powys, a writer whose literary affinities with Forster would repay exploration.

But the finest of these tales, and Forster's last completed work of fiction, is 'The Other Boat'. Begun in 1913, the first part was published in *The Listener* in 1948, as 'Entrance to an Unwritten Novel'. It was completed ten years later. But, despite this piecemeal mode of composition, it has the austerely encouraging quality of consistent art. Here the themes and preoccupations of the earlier stories are put to a serious and fully worked-out purpose. The sexual relationship between the callow young army officer and the devious but devoted half-caste becomes the focus for a study of all the barriers, sexual, ethical and racial, which separate man from man. The other voyagers on this second passage to India, while belonging to the Sawston world, are not caricatured. But Mrs March, the officer's mother, wronged but avenging, is the culmination of all the dominant females in the earlier books. The moment when Lionel invokes her image on the deck, after his quarrel with Cocoanut, is terrifying.

But behind Isabel, behind the Army, was another power, whom he could not consider calmly: his mother, blind-eyed in the midst of the enormous web she had spun – filaments drifting everywhere, strands catching. There was no reasoning with her or about her, she understood nothing and controlled everything. She had suffered too much and was too high-minded to be judged like other people, she was outside carnality and incapable of pardoning it. Earlier in the evening, when Cocoa mentioned her, he had tried to imagine her with his father, enjoying the sensations he was beginning to find so pleasant, but the attempt was sacrilegious and he was shocked at himself. From the great blank country she inhabited came a voice condemning him and all her children for sin, but condemning him most.

Forster had never written quite so forcefully as here: gone are all the rhetorical decorations and manoeuvrings, all the uncertainties and whimsical self-mockery. Mrs March has become a figure of archetypal terror and the embodiment of an attitude to life that (figuratively) slays young men by thousands.

The quarrel with Cocoanut is precisely rendered: the issue of the latter's allowing the cabin door to remain unlocked while the young men are making love embodies two ways of life, two attitudes, of doing and being. And the final resolution, Lionel's suicide, following the murder of his lover, while sombre and almost despairing, still leaves room for the sardonic comedy of the final paragraphs.

In 'The Other Boat' Forster vindicates the approach to sexuality which he has employed in the earlier stories. He does indeed provide a new slant on the age-old question of how to reconcile one's private fantasies and urges with the requirements of the societies and communities in which we live. The element of play, inseparable as Forster sees it, from the kind of love-making he envisages allows him to 'take the heat off', to avoid the element of preaching that we find in, for example, the more strenuous declarations of Lawrence. Freedom from the pressures (though also from the consolations) of children and family life, although the aspect of homosexual love which may account for what seems its frequent irresponsibility, is put to good literary and moral purpose here. Forster, the anatomiser of the idealistic, maintains that sex in isolation can be funny and that no life is ever quite immune from its demands. And he maintains this without recourse to psychological knowingness, without invoking Freud and the secular counterparts of patristic demonology. His Mediterranean dream of spontaneity remained for him the moral touchstone he had found it to be from the start of his literary career.

10   *A Passage to India*

I

The writing of *A Passage to India* was preceded by a lengthy period of literary dithering and false starts. Following the success of *Howards End*, the thirty-year-old author resumed that novel's theme, this time setting out to explore the idealistic division between the Schlegel sisters as it might affect two men. Martin Whitby the intellectual, Cyril Marsh the man of action – what should happen to them? The book hung fire; Forster went to India; and returned with a new novel already partly written, inspired by his experiences there. Again there was a hitch. Then followed the visit to Edward Carpenter at Milthorpe and the writing of *Maurice*. With this therapeutic activity behind him Forster made a fresh start on the novel about the man of action and the intellectual, which he called 'Arctic Summer'. But he could still not get it working, and the Great War arrived and finished it off forever.

The fact that Forster later read extracts from it at the Aldeburgh Festival shows that he was not ashamed of it as it stood. The trouble seems to have been that the issues he had raised in *Maurice* and the urgency he had rediscovered in writing it could not be accommodated by a novel employing previous characters and settings. Italy, an English public school called Radipole (named symbolically after the backwater at Weymouth?), a country house on the Howards End model: they would no longer serve him. The book dissolved in his mind, and the names of Clesant March, the second version of his hero, were dispersed to 'Dr Woolacott' and 'The Other Boat'.

India was of course to be his subject; but not until his residence at Dewas Senior and his relationship with Bapu Sahib the Maharajah had renewed his powers of assimilation and of organising his experience. But he had an indirect ancestral connection with India as well. Among the many charitable

146

bodies supported by his great-uncle Henry Thornton was the Church Missionary Society, one founded to propagate the tenets of evangelical Christianity; and to further its aims the Clapham Sect succeeded in securing Parliamentary approval for the establishment of Christian missions to India. The irony is neat: for it was with Thornton money that Forster was able to visit that country for himself, and to become the most famous writer to attack British policy in India in the 1920s.

Not surprisingly, he diagnosed the situation there in terms of personalities: 'The decent Anglo-Indian of today realizes that the great blunder of the past is neither political nor economic nor educational but social; that he was associated with a system that supported rudeness in railway carriages and is paying the penalty.'[1] This approach may seem trivial and reductive; but it was seriously meant. Forster knew India from having lived and worked there, if only for seven months; and he tried to approach Indian affairs from the point of view of an insider. He knew that life is lived from minute to minute, and that political confrontations are the result of years of undetected personal incidents, and grow up like a coral reef. His interest in the affairs of the sub-continent lasted all his life. He wrote many articles on a variety of Indian subjects, broadcast to India both during and after the Second World War, and returned there in 1945 as an emissary of the PEN Club. He did not simply use the country for fictional copy.

But perhaps for this very reason *A Passage to India* has been treated as a would-be authoritative statement on Indian affairs, and criticised accordingly. For example, Nirad C. Chaudhuri, who in 1959 himself published a not-uncritical account of Forster's own country, under the title *A Passage to England,* has claimed that Forster's picture distorts the reality, being based too exclusively on his experience of the Native States, which represent only a small proportion of the whole.[2] But as G. K. Das demonstrates in his useful study *E. M. Forster's India* (1977), Forster was not ignorant of Indian political movements, and indeed was drawing on recent history in his account of the anti-British disturbances in Chandrapore. Whole incidents and remarks are lifted from contemporary reports. The question of the date of the events recorded elsewhere in the novel is, however, uncertain. Rose Macaulay maintained that the setting is pre-First World War (that is, contemporary with Forster's first

visit to India).[3] Forster himself admits that 'assuredly the novel
dates'. But he went on to assert that 'my main purpose was not
political, was not even sociological'.[4] Certainly the omission of
any reference to the nationalist movements, so prominent at the
time of his second visit, supports this claim: he preferred to treat
them, in Das's phrase, 'like noises off'. For the kind of novel he
was writing, India, as he himself experienced it, was to become
the symbol of the cosmos against which his fictional drama was
to be played: the book does in this respect compare with another
distinguished novel, L. H. Myers's tetralogy *The Near and the
Far* (1931–40), which uses the historical situation in India at the
time of Akbar for contemporary reference. Indeed, just as Forster's early novels can be read in the light of his later maturity and
thus undervalued, so *A Passage to India* can be mistakenly
interpreted in the light of his subsequent political statements and
reprehended for the absence of merits to which it lays no claim.

None the less this novel does embody more than a private
vision: it puts forward the views of a Cambridge liberal as
against the official policy of government and political parties. As
Das comments,

> If Liberal politics centred its aim and attention around the form
> of the government of India and its relationship with the British
> Government, Forster based his own considerations on indi-
> vidual and social life in India and on the relationship between
> individual Indians and Englishmen, and between their two
> communities.[5]

Forster's 'Only connect' is both prescribed for the Indian situation and tested by it. He does not seek to impose English ideas on
India, but submits them to the challenge of India in its totality of
climate, and social and religious diversity, and ancient wisdom.
Perhaps it is his stress on antiquity which now alienates modern
Indians – that and what even so sympathetic a critic as Das feels
to be his patronising treatment of Hinduism. Certainly he himself acknowledged that he found Islam more congenial.

The patronising tone may also be detected, more forgivably, in
the letters which he wrote to his mother from the court at Dewas
Senior, and which were published in *The Hill of Devi* (1953), an
invaluable supplement to any reading of the novel, and one
which provides originals for a number of its incidents and

symbols. The early letters especially are, on his own admission, 'too prone to turn remote and rare matters into suburban jokes'; but what soon emerges as most significant is Forster's love and reverence for the Maharajah himself, whose life was, like the so-different life of Rickie Elliot, to end in ruin. 'He will go down to history as a failure. That is the sort of thing that does go down to history.'[6] But, for Forster, Bapu Sahib was a saint.

> When I returned to England and he heard that I was worried because the post-war world of the 20s would not add up into sense, he sent me a message. 'Tell him,' it ran, 'tell him from me to follow his heart and his mind will see everything clear.' The message as phrased is too facile: doors open into silliness at once. But to remember and respect and prefer the heart, to have the instinct which follows it whenever possible – what surer help than that could one have through life?[7]

The qualification is typical; but the question, if rhetorical, had been tried and not found wanting. In the persons of Mrs Moore and Dr Aziz, Forster was to submit the Maharajah's advice to the challenge of the country which had fathered it.

That he should do so is evidence also of his continuing personal preoccupation. The situation between English and Indian provided an emotional parallel and, in imaginative terms, an emotional surrogate, for the relations between homosexual and heterosexual in contemporary society. As George Steiner observes,

> The choice of theme and treatment in Forster's masterpiece . . . represents an act of sublimation. . . . By translating his locale to India and to the social discriminations between raj and native, Forster can now express the full gamut of his protest against snobbery, against the shallow cruelty of status and inherited privilege. . . .

And he goes on to point out that 'The non-event in the hills of Marabar comprises values that we can now confidently recognize as being both heterosexual and homosexual. Both are facets, momentary and – it may be – contingent, of the unbounded unity of love.'[8]

II

The central incident of *A Passage to India* is so enthralling that it tends to obscure the less dramatic but no less significant events that follow. The trial of Dr Aziz is over with the final quarter of the novel yet to run; and it is that portion which tends to be forgotten when one looks back upon the book. The brief third section, 'Temple', can feel like an anti-climax or an afterthought; and it even seems designed as one. At the end of his meditation during the feast of the birth of Krishna, all that Professor Godbole has managed to retrieve is 'One old Englishwoman and one little, little wasp. . . . It does not seem much, still it is more than I am myself.'

The old woman is the most haunting character in this rich and complex novel. By the end of the book she has become a minor deity, Esmiss Esmoor; but at the start she is merely Mrs Moore from Northamptonshire, twice married and twice widowed, who has brought Miss Adela Quested out to India so that she can decide whether she wishes to marry Mrs Moore's eldest son, Ronny Heaslop, City Magistrate of the town of Chandrapore. Adela is the well-meaning Englishwoman visitor determined to 'see India' – in the abstract. But to see India one must meet Indians, and this the inhabitants of the British enclave in Chandrapore refuse to do. Mrs Moore, however, has a chance meeting in a mosque with Dr Aziz, an emotional but highly intelligent young Moslem; and as a result he escorts the two women to see the celebrated Marabar caves a few miles outside the city. The expedition is a disaster. Mrs Moore suffers a species of breakdown after entering the first cave, and Adela, after entering another, accuses Aziz of trying to assault her. His trial is the occasion for race riots and a display of doctrinaire loyalty on the part of the English, who automatically assume his guilt, his only white supporter being the headmaster of the English College, Cyril Fielding. But at the trial Adela withdraws the charge and the case collapses. She is ostracised, her engagement is broken off, and she returns to England. The friendship between Fielding and Aziz is seriously damaged, and, when the former takes a wife, Aziz assumes bitterly that it is Miss Quested. The final revelation that she is Mrs Moore's daughter Stella only partly heals the breach. The friendship, like the understanding between

Englishmen and Indians generally, must be postponed to an indefinite future.

As can be seen, it is the contact between individuals and the clash of character which form the substance of the book. The groupings are distinct: a cluster of English, a cluster of Indians, and between them four people who are all concerned in their different ways with reconciliation – Aziz, Fielding, Adela and Mrs Moore. But all the characters are subordinate to a psychic–physical world that is both India and the enormous chaos of life itself.

On a first reading the English would appear to receive short shrift, and when the book came out there were indignant protests that the portrait of them was unfair. The caustic tone with which they are described, the narrow-mindedness, snobbery and bigotry they show towards the Indians, alienate us from the very start; at the same time the witty precision with which Forster makes his points all but endears them to us for being its occasion. The anger is thus offset by literary skill. And on a closer reading it becomes apparent that it is the women who are the chief offenders: Mrs Turton, Mrs McBryde and the rest are straight out of Sawston and, one feels, will probably retire there.

But the men are differentiated: the weary, scrupulously honest Turton; McBryde the policeman (whose adultery, with the very woman who has encouraged Adela to proffer charges against Aziz, is a happy touch of irony); Aziz's superior the brutal surgeon Major Callendar. The most interesting of them is Ronny, Mrs Moore's son: for all his limitations of imagination and sympathy he is a rounded character, understood by the author and to some extent the object of his sympathy. He is the vicitim of a whole social, not to say imperial, system, which has made him what he is.

The English are, however, more interesting in the mass than as individuals. Their reaction to the affair of the Marabar Caves is exactly caught.

They had started speaking of 'women and children' – that phrase that exempts the male from sanity when it has been repeated a few times. Each felt that all he loved best in the world was at stake, demanded revenge, and was filled with a not unpleasing glow, in which the chilly and half-known features of Miss Quested vanished, and were replaced by all that is sweetest and warmest in the private life. 'But it's the women and children,' they repeated, and the Collector knew that he ought to stop them intoxicating themselves, but he hadn't the heart.   (Ch. 20)

The scene at the Club when Fielding, after trying to stand up for reason, is turned out, is an example of Forster's dramatic writing at its best. (Objections to its implausibility were to be raised, however, and not only by indignant Anglo-Indians.[9])

The Indians, if less immediately vivid, are at the heart of the book. There are quite a number of them, and they are unobtrusively deployed to demonstrate the range of Indian life and its complexity, and the variety of its social and religious customs. The Moslems are central here. Dramatically this is appropriate, for Islam is close enough to Christianity to provide a dynamic opposition to the English. Aziz has his own close friends: Hamidullah the barrister, respectable, balanced, but embittered by the harm that the attitude and personalities of the English community have produced; and Mahmoud Ali, more volatile and violent, but whom Aziz values despite his malevolent interference between him and Fielding, and whose offences he forgives 'because he loved me'. There is the Nawab Bahadur, the leading Mohammedan landowner, with his disreputable grandson Nureddin – the type of scamp with whom Forster would seem to have had a sneaking sympathy. The presence of the Nawab appears to cause divisiveness; it is in his car that Adela and Ronny so unfortunately reconcile their differences, and at his house that suspicion of Fielding is sown in Aziz's mind following the trial.

The Hindus are, until the third part of the novel, seen at one remove, through Moslem eyes. But we feel them to be the real representatives of India, beside whom even the Moslems are newcomers. Aziz's fantasies about his ancestors, the conquerors, only go to make this more plain. Hinduism also provides both the challenge and the resolution in the novel: as Forster wrote, 'It is true that Hinduism emphasizes the fact that we are all different. But it also emphasizes the other side of the human paradox – the fact that we are all the same.'[10]

Professor Godbole is the most prominent Hindu in the book, and it is his song to Krishna which helps to begin the disturbance of the visitors' tranquillity. Things are never to be the same for either woman after their tea party at Fielding's house.

His thin voice rose and gave out one sound after another. At times there seemed rhythm, at times there was the illusion of a Western melody. But the ear, baffled repeatedly, soon lost any clue, and wandered in a maze of noises, none harsh or unpleasant, none intelligible. It was the song of an unknown bird.   (Ch. 7)

It is Godbole's miscalculation of the length of a prayer which causes him and Fielding to miss the train on the Marabar expedition; and, again characteristically, he leaves Chandrapore as soon as trouble starts. Always detached, he is none the less at the heart of the action. The reality which he knows and in his way enunciates is the dimension of mystery which in the end engulfs the novel.

The difference between Englishmen and Indians is apparent at every turn; and the friendship between Fielding and Aziz founders on it. Here we have the heart of the book's humanistic message. It is not surprising, this being a Forster novel, that the relationship should be short-lived and tenuous: what gives it force is the sensed desire on each side that it should continue, and also a tenderness that borders on, without crossing over into, the erotic: small touches, intimacies, achieve a lot here. Very characteristic is the episode of the collar stud. While dressing for the ominous tea-party Fielding loses his stud, and Aziz lends him his own, which is, he claims, a spare. It is a gold one, 'part of a set that his brother-in-law had brought him from Europe. . . . Replacing his collar, he prayed that it would not spring up at the back during tea.' Later on Ronny, escorting the ladies on their cantankerous journey to the Maidan remarks, 'Aziz was exquisitely dressed, from tie-pin to spats, but he had forgotten his back collar-stud, and there you have the Indian all over: inattention to detail; the fundamental slackness that reveals the race' (Ch. 8). This sets up a jangle in Adela's nerves, which causes her, wisely, to decide not to marry him. Later they take a ride in the Nawab's car, and are involved in the mysterious accident on the Marabar road which results in their reconciliation. And it is the continued confusion in Adela's mind which leads to the false charge and to Aziz's imprisonment. The narrative proceeds on numerous small links of this kind, which induce a feeling of mysterious fatality.

Certainly fate draws Fielding and Aziz apart. The former's championship of his friend is offset by his allowing Adela to take refuge in the College during the riots: there is enough enmity towards the English for some of it to spill over even onto the trusted Fielding. He is a shadowy figure, known more in his attitude to others than in his attitude to himself: it is Aziz and not the author who refers to him as 'Cyril'. His self-sufficiency and resolution make him an uncharacteristic Forster hero. His marriage to Stella Moore, despite the troubling hint as to the partial frustration of his middle-aged desires, promises more fulfilment than Forster usually allows his characters. But, if Fielding's ostracism by the Club draws its strength from the author's own sensitivity to society's ostracism of the homosexual and from his dread of being at the mercy of 'the gang', so the uneasy relationship between him and his wife hints at the predicament of those for whom sexual awakening comes too late. There is a disturbing ambiguity in this aspect of the conclusion, just as there is in the final reconciliation with Aziz.

Aziz himself is certainly the most memorable of the male characters; and this not surprisingly, since he is based both on Forster's friend Syed Ross Masood and on his lover Mohammed el Adl. With his volatility and warmth, his sudden angers and sulks, his courtesy and loving heart, he has a spontaneity that is itself a criticism of the inhibitions of the English. That those inhibitions are in part the creation of a position of authority is shown in Forster's comment on Turton's words, when the Collector interviews Fielding after the return from Marabar: '"I have had twenty-five years experience of this country" – he paused, and "twenty-five years" seemed to fill the waiting-room with their staleness and ungenerosity . . .' (Ch. 17). But Aziz lives in the present, evolving his realities as he goes.

It may be felt that Forster patronises him: certainly there is humour at his expense in a way that we do not find, for example, in Joyce Cary's treatment of the eponymous hero of *Mister Johnson* (1939). The preparations for the picnic are a case in point.

Aziz was terribly worried. It was not a long expedition – a train left Chandrapore just before dawn, another would bring them back for tiffin – but he was only a little official still, and feared to acquit himself dishonourably. He had to ask Major

Callendar for half a day's leave, and he refused because of his recent malingering; despair; renewed approach of Major Callendar through Fielding, and contemptuous snarling permission. He had to borrow cutlery from Mahmoud Ali without inviting him. Then there was the question of alcohol; Mr Fielding, and perhaps the ladies, were drinkers, so must he provide whisky-sodas and ports? There was the problem of transport from the wayside station of Marabar to the caves. There was the problem of Professor Godbole and his food, and of Professor Godbole and other people's food – two problems, not one problem. The Professor was not a very strict Hindu – he would take tea, fruit, and soda-water and sweets, whoever cooked them, and vegetables and rice if cooked by a Brahman; but not meat, not cakes lest they contained eggs, and he would not allow anyone else to eat beef: a slice of beef upon a distant plate would wreck his happiness. Other people might eat mutton, they might eat ham. But over ham Aziz's own religion raised its voice: he did not fancy other people eating ham. Trouble after trouble encountered him, because he had challenged the spirit of the Indian earth, which tries to keep men in compartments.   (Ch. 13)

The last sentence deprives the account of the satire of which it seems at first to consist: it also illumines Forster's own choice of India for a subject. The whole passage compares with the account of Philip and Harriet's journey across Italy in *Where Angels Fear to Tread*; its high-spirited celebration of disorganisation and the chaotic has a curiously liberating effect.

Aziz's experiences during his arrest and imprisonment derive from a similar misadventure (though one arising from a different cause) which befell Forster's friend Mohammed in Egypt. Perhaps it is because of this that we never see Aziz alone in prison. But there are good additional reasons for this: the reader is withdrawn from him, as though deprived of the right to companion him. The view we have of him through other people's eyes is endearing, and wins our respect. We know him as the friend of Mrs Moore and Fielding. Above all Aziz is important as an example of the influence of Western individual consciousness upon India. The future, Forster would seem to suggest, is with him rather than with Godbole; though that which Godbole knows and represents will always be there. Aziz's decision to regard the English as his enemies is the more tragic.

That tragedy is a result of a blunder out of the Schlegel world. In *Howards End* we hear of a Miss Quested who 'plays'; and Adela has a certain resemblance to Margaret Schlegel, though she lacks her sensitivity. She too is plain, honest, outspoken, well-intentioned. She wishes to know India; but the India she finds proves overwhelming. By an unpleasant irony the English community is proved right: the curiosity they deplore has disastrous results. Adela's subsequent ostracism, and the universal disapproval she encounters arouse our sympathy for a character hitherto unattractive. Nor does Forster use her satirically. He is more interested in her relations with Ronny than in her desire to know India. It is the muddle in her own heart which is at the root of the subsequent mischief.

For Adela is prepared to enter into that dark night of the spirit that awaited Lucy Honeychurch: she will pretend to love where love does not exist. The movements in her mind are subtly presented; but in addition India too affects her decision – or her lack of one. At Fielding's tea-party she hears herself announcing that she will shortly be leaving the country: the decision has been taken without her knowing it. This revelation of the power of her unconscious mind alarms her; but on the Maidan (the playing field, where action is simple and spontaneous, witness the encounter between Aziz and the polo-playing subaltern) she speaks frankly to Ronny, and the right decision is unemotionally but correctly made. Then the Nawab invites them for a ride in his new car, choosing the Gangavati road. He proceeds to fall asleep, and Ronny instructs the driver to take them along the Marabar road, as having the better surfacee. On that road they collide with a mysterious animal in the dark, which disappears after causing the car to run into a tree. The Nawab is distraught because, we learn later, he believes this to be a ghost seeking his life. But the unlucky event has the effect of drawing Ronny and Adela together in a moment of spurious fellowship. They are given a lift back to Chandrapore by the sprightly Miss Derek – who is to give Adela another lift a few days later after her panic-stricken flight from the caves. The parallel helps us to link the hallucinatory experience of the accident with her experience in the cave. And the latter is, as Forster suggests, the result of muddle in her own mind.

For what does happen in the cave? Before she enters, Adela

has been talking to Aziz about his marriage but thinking about her own. The resulting distraction causes her to ask him, with unintentional offensiveness,

'Have you one wife or more than one?'
The question shocked the young man very much. It chal-lenged a new conviction of his community, and new convic-tions are more sensitive than old. If she had said, 'Do you worship one god or several?' he would not have objected. But to ask an educated Indian Moslem how many wives he has – appalling, hideous! He was in trouble how to conceal his confusion. 'One, one in my own particular case,' he splut-tered, and let go of her hand. Quite a number of caves were at the top of the track, and thinking, 'Damn the English even at their best,' he plunged into one of them to recover his balance. She followed at her leisure, quite unconscious that she had said the wrong thing, and not seeing him, she also went into a cave, thinking with half her mind 'sight-seeing bores me,' and wondering with the other half about marriage.   (Ch. 15)

A condition of complete muddle is in operation: even Aziz's reply is a lie, for his wife is dead. Animosity, failure of response, boredom, thoughtlessness: the mental ground is ready for dis-aster.

What happens after that we never know, nor apparently did Forster himself. Was Adela attacked by the guide? or by another Indian? or by her own outraged sexual self? The answer is in the end irrelevant: though it is noteworthy that Aziz is said to have waited in his cave 'a minute' before going out to look for her. Whatever happened happened in an extremely short space of time. But we are beyond the proper concerns of objective verifica-tion. All that we do know is that, whatever the cave harboured, the connection between it and Adela's state of mind was magne-tic. And her neglect of her true self results in delusion and collapse. Not the least telling moment in the novel occurs during the trial when, in answer to McBryde's assertion that 'the darker races are physically attracted to the fairer, but not *vice versa*', a rude voice calls, 'Even when the lady is so much uglier than the gentleman?' The humour of this is soon checked. 'But the comment had upset Miss Quested. Her body resented being called ugly, and trembled.' That bestowal of autonomy upon the body is most effective, not least because Adela's plainness is remarked on more than once. By means such as this Forster engages our sympathy with her, indeed our pity. She never receives her due for the courage of her recantation from anyone except Fielding.

As to that recantation itself, it arises out of the clarity of mind induced in her by the crowd's chant of 'Esmiss Esmoor'; Mrs Moore become a goddess, Mrs Moore who, unknown to Adela, is dead, but whose spirit, blessed with the second thoughts on India with which she embarked for home, permeates the air with reconciliation. It is one of the most beautiful yet elusive moments in Forster's work, elusive because disguised by a protective irony and humour that are very typical. But beautiful it is.

A further irony in this perfectly controlled ironic novel is the fact that the one person who becomes a goddess does nothing at all. Aziz from his first encounter with Mrs Moore in the mosque (the magic of that scene never seems to stale) loves her unreservedly and for ever; and her presence pervades the book. Why? It is hard to say. An elderly lady without any obvious wit or charm, she is nearly as colourless as Mrs Wilcox; but like Mrs Wilcox she has an instinctive feeling for human needs which is at home in the Orient – or indeed anywhere. She removes her shoes outside the mosque, not because she has been told to do so but as a matter of course: it is this which wins Aziz's heart and which makes him call her an Oriental. She is direct and sincere and sensible; but she is not romanticised.

> Going to hang up her cloak, she found that the tip of the peg was occupied by a small wasp. She had known this wasp or his relatives by day; they were not as English wasps, but had long yellow legs which hung down behind when they flew. Perhaps he mistook the peg for a branch – no Indian animal has any sense of an interior. Bats, rats, birds, insects will as soon nest inside a house as out; it is to them a normal growth of the eternal jungle, which alternately produces houses trees, houses trees. There he clung, asleep while jackals in the plain bayed their desires and mingled with the percussion of drums.   (Ch. 3)

Forster frequently takes the opportunity provided by moments like this to evoke the casual boundlessness of India, and to suggest that the interior 'civilised' life is also 'a normal growth of the eternal jungle'. And both wasp and jackal will be taken up again two pages on, when we are told of the speculations of the two Christian missionaries about the admission of animals to Heaven, a passage which looks forward to the great vision of inclusion at the end of the book.

> May there not be a mansion for the monkeys also? Old Mr Graysford said No, but young Mr Sorley, who was advanced, said Yes; he saw no reason why monkeys should not have their collateral share of bliss, and he had sympathetic discussions about them with his Hindu friends. And the jackals? Jackals were indeed less to Mr Sorley's mind, but he admitted that the mercy of God, being infinite, may well embrace all mammals. And the wasps? He became uneasy during the descent to wasps, and was apt to change the conversation. And oranges, cactuses, crystals and mud? and the bacteria inside Mr Sorley? No, no, this is going too far. We must exclude someone from our gathering, or we shall be left with nothing.   (Ch. 4)

Here the difference between East and West is beautifully and philosophically pointed up: the claims of inclusiveness and exclusiveness are played off against each other throughout the novel. Mrs Moore is not inclined to the exclusive view: '"Pretty dear," said Mrs Moore to the wasp. He did not wake, but her voice floated out, to swell the night's uneasiness' (Ch. 3). A lesser novelist, perhaps any other novelist but Forster, instead of 'uneasiness' would have written 'calm'.

But Mrs Moore is no idealised figure: already by the time of Fielding's tea-party she has begun to feel weary and old. She undertakes the Marabar expedition out of a courteous sense of duty. And her entry into the first cave nearly marks the end of her. The experience is dealt with in a matter-of-fact way, and the reasons for her terror listed – overcrowding, heat, smells, a baby's naked body pressed onto her face in the dark; but the real cause of the trouble, the echo, is inexplicable, though Forster does his best to indicate its meaning as well as its effect.

> The crush and the smells she could forget, but the echo began in some indescribable way to undermine her hold on life.

> Coming at a moment when she chanced to be fatigued, it had
> managed to murmur, 'Pathos, piety, courage – they exist, but
> are identical, and so is filth. Everything exists, nothing has
> value.'   (Ch. 14)

Here is the inclusiveness of India registered negatively by a
Western mind: that it should be Mrs Moore's mind makes the
sense of difference between East and West all the more telling.
The effect on her is to eliminate all desire; life is an indifferent
weariness, and everything only echoes 'boum'.

> Devils are of the North, and poems can be written about them,
> but no one could romanticize the Marabar because it robbed
> infinity and eternity of their vastness, the only quality that
> accommodates them to mankind.

This is, of course, the attitude of the West, and its vulnerability
to an experience which is not necessarily peculiar to the East is
developed in the account of Mrs Moore's final breakdown.

> She had come to that state where the horror of the universe and
> its smallness are both visible at the same time – the twilight of
> the double vision in which so many elderly people are in-
> volved. If this world is not to our taste, well, at all events there
> is Heaven, Hell, Annihilation – one or other of those large
> things, that huge scenic background of stars, fires, blue or
> black air. All heroic endeavour, and all that is known as art,
> assumes that there is such a background, just as all practical
> endeavour, when the world is to our taste, assumes that the
> world is all. But in the twilight of the double vision, a spiritual
> muddledom is set up for which no high-sounding words can be
> found; we can neither act nor refrain from action, we can
> neither ignore nor respect Infinity.   (Ch. 23)

This spiritual muddledom is something that Forster has been
examining in all his earlier novels; but here he relates it to a more
general concept, to the very religious sense itself. *A Passage to
India* is well named: it is the journey from Western ideas of
choice, selection, organisation, materialism into the formless
chaos of life which challenges all these categories and which,
most important of all, tests Western notions of the Absolute.

Mrs Moore, good, ordinary lady, is the perfect medium for the encounter. For all her differences from Adela Quested, she complements her. If Adela's sense of her conscious choosing self is shattered, her older companion knows an annihilation that goes deeper still.

Mrs Moore had always inclined to resignation. As soon as she landed in India it seemed to her good, and when she saw the water flowing through the mosque-tank, or the Ganges, or the moon, caught in the shawl of night with all the other stars, it seemed a beautiful goal and an easy one. To be one with the universe! So dignified and simple. But there was always some little duty to be performed first, some new card to be turned up from the diminishing pack and placed, and while she was pottering about, the Marabar struck its gong.

This is Forster's version of the Advent message of judgement and eternity.

Once the Marabar expedition is over, Mrs Moore, like Rickie Elliot, 'deteriorates'. It is one of the most honest and disturbing things in the book that she should do so, that she should become a peevish, self-centred old woman. She ceases to be of use, for nothing matters to her any more. So she is shipped off home, and dies at sea. Our last glimpse of her, however, offsets her earlier despair: the sight of other parts of India brings an alternative, strengthening sense of relativity. 'So you thought an echo was India, you took the Marabar caves as final?' *All* absolutes can become idols. India eclipses Howards End and Abinger just as it eclipsed Grasmere for Adela and Ronny. Indeed, Mrs Moore's collapse can be read as Forster's own critique of his use of Mrs Wilcox as a symbol. Even the wise mother, the Demeter figure, is put to the test and found wanting. And yet even that is not the whole truth. Mrs Moore presides over the novel as she rules in Aziz's heart – or, rather, *because* she rules in Aziz's heart: it is his love for her which confers such high value upon her. It is through appealing to her memory that Fielding persuades Aziz to let Adela off lightly following the trial. Down-to-earth but sensitive, quiet but knowing her own mind, Mrs Moore is the keystone of the book, and it is she who makes the important distinction, noted above, between a mystery and a muddle.

The muddle here is everywhere, in Adela's emotions, in the

English attitude to their role in India, above all in Chandrapore itself. The opening description prepares us for what is to follow.

> Edged rather than washed by the River Ganges, it trails for a couple of miles along the bank, scarcely distinguishable from the rubbish it deposits so freely. There are no bathing-steps on the river front, as the Ganges happens not to be holy there; indeed there is no river front, and bazaars shut out the wide and shifting panorama of the stream. The streets are mean, the temples ineffective, and though a few fine houses exist they are hidden away in gardens or down alleys whose filth deters all but the invited guest. . . . There is no painting and scarcely any carving in the bazaars. The very wood seems made of mud, the inhabitants of mud moving. So abased, so monotonous is everything that meets the eye, that when the Ganges comes down it might be expected to wash the excrescence back into the soil. Houses do fall, people are drowned and left rotting, but the general outline of the town persists, swelling here, shrinking there, like some low but indestructible form of life.   (Ch. 1)

India does indeed provide Forster with his objective correlative, embodied here in a muddle too vast for the rational mind to comprehend. If it repels Sawston minds like the 'Turtons and Burtons' (as Aziz's friends contemptuously call them) it overwhelms the more sensitive Schlegel type. It is muddle on such a scale as to constitute a mystery.

Forster's response to the Indian landscape is altogether different from his rather literary evocations of England. In an essay reprinted in *Abinger Harvest* he conveys with simplicity and unobtrusive skill the fascination which the drab Indian landscape held for him:

> The plain lacks the romance of solitude. Desolate at the first glance, it conceals numberless groups of a few men. The grasses and the high crops sway, the distant path undulates, and is barred with brown bodies or heightened with saffron and crimson. In the evening the villages stand out and call to one another across emptiness with drums and fires. This clump of trees was apparently a village, for near the few men was a sort of enclosure surrounding a kind of street, and gods

multiplied. The ground was littered with huts and rubbish for a few yards, and then the plain resumed; to continue in its gentle confusion as far as the eye could see.[11]

This sense of non-romantic strangeness pervades the novel too. The account of the Marabar Hills carefully avoids any 'heightening' in Gothic terms, getting its effects by an awareness of distortion which is surrealistic in its effect.

The elephant walked straight at the Kawa Dol as if she would knock for admission with her forehead, then swerved, and followed a path round its base. The stones plunged straight into the earth, like cliffs into the sea, and while Miss Quested was remarking on this, and saying that it was striking, the plain quietly disappeared, peeled off, so to speak, and nothing was to be seen on either side but the granite, very dead and quiet. The sky dominated as usual, but seemed unhealthily near, adhering like a ceiling to the summits of the precipices. It was as if the contents of the corridor had never been changed.   (Ch. 14)

The effect here is of a landscape full of withheld movement – and of hostile movement. The emphasis is on solidity, substantiality, not on colour, scent or fluctuations of light (there is none possible in this glare of day).

Everything seemed cut off at its root, and therefore infected with illusion. For instance, there were some mounds by the edge of the track, low, serrated, and touched with whitewash. What were these mounds – graves, breasts of the goddess Parvati? The villagers beneath gave both replies. Again, there was a confusion about a snake which was never cleared up. Miss Quested saw a thin, dark object reared on end at the farther side of a water-course, and said 'A snake!' The villagers agreed, and Aziz explained: yes, a black cobra, very venomous, who had reared himself up to watch the passing of the elephant. But when she looked through Ronny's field-glasses, she found it wasn't a snake, but the withered and twisted stump of a toddy-palm. So she said, 'It isn't a snake.' The villagers contradicted her. She had put the word into their minds, and they refused to abandon it.

The journey prefigures the world of delusion and total relativity that issues from the caves.

The caves have something in common with the question mark which George Emerson scrawls on the piece of paper pinned to the wash-stand in *A Room with a View* (that particular colloca- tion is typical of Forster's imagination). What is emphasised about them is that they contain nothing; empty, they provide echoes and reflections only. This withdrawal of meaning swal- lows up the two women, one old and tired, the other one confused, into its vacuum. The fact that Mrs Moore is a victim of what lies before the emergence of meaning and rationality and spiritual beauty does not invalidate the values which she em- bodies: the physical reason for her collapse is itself a modifica- tion of whatever sinister message the caves may contain. But the civilised life is seen as something hard-won, perpetually menaced, and always liable to be drawn back into the mud from which it arose. There is a parallel here with Arthur Machen's vision of evil as retrogressive evolution; but also with the sober optimism of Forster's venerated Lowes Dickinson. The 'violence and vulgarity' of Europe lead back to the nullity waiting in the Caves. The Caves are indeed a Forsterian equivalent of Hardy's Egdon Heath, the demonstration that, whatever ideals of love and fellowship humanity may cherish, nature herself is indiffer- ent to them. They represent a reality which it is impossible for all but the very wise to bear. Only panic and emptiness await the spiritual materialist who comes in contact with it.

In the closing section of the book the muddle of India is united with its mystery. Forster himself said that the Hindu festival of the birth of Krishna may be regarded as the scene in the cave 'turned inside out'.[12] Godbole's meditation and the cheerful mess of the festival itself bring together the chaotic elements in an acceptance of disorder that amounts to a re-ordering. Mrs Moore and the wasp (a wasp or the wasp: it is all one in the total reality that is Krishna) – these come to his mind; and this process of unity through chance is itself to be found at work in the fabric of the novel. The episode of the snake, quoted above, is recollected, or rather echoed, in Godbole's discussion of the viper found in one of the College rooms immediately after the arrest of Aziz; and the uncertainty concerning the reptile's presence is taken up into Godbole's own discussion of the nature of good and evil, their omnipresence and copresence as aspects of Krishna. Again, the tracks in the Marabar road after the collision of the Nawab's car with an unknown beast are brought to Adela's mind as she sees the footholds nicked in the rock on the way up to the caves: once again she is muddling about over her relationship with Ronny. Even the accident itself is repeated at the same place, when Nureddin drives Aziz into the ditch following his release on bail – which reopens the whole question of its supernatural origin. And all these images and motifs are taken up into the repeated cry, the cry to Krishna the Lord of Life, of Good and Evil, an invocation of necessary but ambiguous character that echoes Maurice Hall's heartfelt cry from his window to the as-yet unknown Alec Scudder.

The invocation of Krishna is an invocation of life in all its wholeness; and where Mosque and Cave, human thought and endeavour and that which they have grown out of, fail to harmonise, the Temple into the infinite may yet achieve the reconciliation. The world of India and its religion become descriptive of a state of complex being such as Western humanism fails to reckon with; and under the muted sadness of the ending, 'No, not yet', and 'No, not there', beyond both space and time a hope is indicated. In part this is mediated through certain isolated figures who suggest a significance that cannot be fully realised. Though very different from those described by Wordsworth in *The Prelude,* they are suggestive of a kindred meaning. The most famous of them is the punkah wallah, whose simple majesty of form rebukes the sordid bustle and acrimony of race prejudice at the trial, suggesting a further dimension of existence altogether; the sight of him clears Adela's mind of its confusion. Or there is that friendly stranger heard near the beginning of the novel as the two weary ladies wait outside the Club.

'Later and later,' yawned Mrs Moore, who was tired after her walk. 'Let me think – don't see the other side of the moon out here, no.'

'Come, India's not as bad as all that,' said a pleasant voice. 'Other side of the earth, if you like, but we stick to the same old moon.' Neither of them knew the speaker nor did they ever see him again. He passed with his friendly word through red-brick pillars into the darkness.   (Ch. 3)

The effect of that passage really is, to use a much-overworked term, magical.

What gives *A Passage to India* its peculiar distinction is the union of its method with its message, a union which anticipates by three years the similar achievement in Virginia Woolf's *To the Lighthouse*: indeed, what Dorothy M. Hoare wrote about that novel applies to this one too, for in it 'art and life are no longer hostile to each other; they both unite in their attempt to achieve perfection of the moment in differing material'.[13] In both cases the inner significance of the book is mediated through an entirely realised physical setting. For Forster's India is real, very real, albeit one that has little of the ferocity or glamour of the India of Rudyard Kipling. It embodies the raw material of life, inescapable and not to be denied, that in its squalor, inefficiency and muddle has yet managed to evolve beauty, courtesy and grace. The narrative, moving easily between the two worlds of the Indians and the English, is notably free from those digressions and comments which are a feature of its predecessors; and such comments as there are relate more to India itself than to manners or morals. The various coincidences are left for the reader to pick up for himself: to cite one instance, the bully who insults Fielding at the Club following Aziz's arrest is the same carefree young subaltern with whom Aziz had earlier played polo on the Maidan, to his contentment and liberation of spirits; another example is Ralph Moore's cry 'Oh, Oh' when he comes upon Aziz in the European Guest House, which echoes his mother's initial exclamation in the mosque and thus paves the way to such reconciliation as the book affords. Wheels within wheels: the novel is full of them, and the three-dimensional nature of the narrative reinforces its overall purpose, itself becoming an image of the attitude of life which it proposes. So far as Forster was able to resolve the contradictions of the world he knew and the ideals he believed in, he resolved them here; which is why, perhaps, *A Passage to India* is not only his finest novel but his last as well.

Conclusion

Forster's position as a resident Honorary Fellow at King's was without precedent, and a sign of the great affection in which he was held by young and old. His status as a senior man of letters seemed unassailable. The modest way in which his small, rather tortoise-like figure moved about the Backs only served to highlight his actual eminence: Forster 'was' Cambridge – or so it seemed. The apostle of gentleness lived on to be a rebuke to the strident 1960s.

He served for a while on the gardening committee, 'though apt, it was said, to be distracted from its deliberations by looking at the flowers'.[1] The anecdote will charm some temperaments but madden others, who will see in it evidence merely of his ineffectiveness and of the sentimentality of the Forster cult. Indeed, so long as he is set up as a great humanist sage Forster will be vulnerable to such criticism; and Lionel Trilling's emphasis on this aspect of his work may turn out to have been a shade misleading: certainly Forster himself wears the robes of consequence with an uneasy air, for the virtues with which his name is associated are essentially virtues of private rather than of public life. When he did speak out, it was from his own experience, and not as a member of a group. Indeed, not only was he an exemplar of Bloomsbury standards at their best – he also anticipated them: they were the things for which he had already learned to live.

But the fact that Forster has spoken with his own brand of unstrained eloquence on behalf of individual rights; that he played an active part in humanist societies; that he could analyse the relationship between personal liberty and social responsibility – all these do not of themselves confer on him prophetic stature; and even *A Passage to India*, impressive though it is, is not a novel of epic grandeur. Forster's real importance lies less in what he said, valid though it was, than in the spirit of undeviating honesty with which he said it, and in the way in which he accepted and remained faithful to his own temperament. The very cessation of his activity as a novelist witnesses to his integrity as man and artist.

For he was first and foremost a creative writer, not a philosopher or journalist or politician; and his occasional publications, the bulk of which appeared after his work in fiction was over, put forward attitudes and convictions developed during his career as a novelist. Rather than censure him for the apparent limitation of his commitment, we should applaud him for engaging in public affairs to the extent he did. For not only did he bring to them a voice and vision that has outlasted those of his more overtly 'committed' contemporaries: he also brought to them the authority of one who was speaking against the grain of his own temperament.

That particular temperament can irritate. The puckish humour, 'the refusal', in Trillings's phrase, 'to be great',² the plain speaking and avoidance of academic and technological jargon – all these things resist his being treated with solemnity. That very element of cosiness which lends so much charm to the early novels and tales can easily belittle the seriousness of what he has to say, and even cancel the impression made when he does speak out. Nor is it necessarily in his favour to realise that these qualities were in part the product of the condition of living single. But the difference between the married (in whatever sense) and the single is arguably more considerable than that between the homosexual and the heterosexual, especially now that we know how much reciprocal crossing of that particular borderline goes on. The outlook of those who are compelled, or who choose, to live with and from themselves inevitably differs from that of people who daily endure, learn from and enjoy each other; but it is not necessarily of less worth. The word 'spinsterly' has been used of Forster (F. R. Leavis employed it no less than three times in his *Scrutiny* essay of 1938): one wonders why it should be a word of disapproval. Unmarried women are not the least selfless or valuable members of the community; while to imply 'of either sex' only rebounds upon the sneerer. Forster challenges our usual assumptions as to what constitutes virility.

The position of liberal humanists is readily accessible to criticism; but, while Forster was well aware that men were not to be dissuaded from preying on each other, he was equally convinced that any doctrine of innate depravity amounted to a denial of the human spirit. His essays on 'What I Believe' (1938), 'The

Challenge of Our Time' (1946) and 'Art for Art's Sake' (1949), the last-named in particular, are the result of the fine balance of values achieved in *A Passage to India*.[3] Certainly the ever-expanding creative potential of art impressed him more than the cramping legislative aspects of morality; and, while careful to distinguish between a belief in the supreme value of art and a belief that only art matters, he always set his face against that creeping philistinism which too often masquerades as social concern. Even the celebrated (or notorious) statement that 'if I had to choose between betraying my country and betraying my friend I hope I should have the guts to betray my country' becomes in this context more than a mere preference for the private life, and equally a recognition that without singularity can be no generality. His outlook is Aristotelian rather than Platonic.

His essays provide us with a working credo for the individual, at once modest and defiant. In pessimistic moments he might have agreed with Lawrence's comment in the letter quoted earlier: 'Forster knows, as every thinking man now knows, that all his thinking and his passion for humanity amounts to no more than trying to soothe with poetry a man raging with pain that cannot be cured.'[4] This admittedly was written at a desperately painful time in Lawrence's own life; but it none the less voices the bedrock situation which every aesthetic theory or preoccupation has sooner or later to face. And yet Lawrence's statement is not so easily assented to as its rhetorical implication might suggest. Certainly, in acknowledging the limitations of art and philanthropy, as of everything else (except love? – but even love can fail, so *A Passage to India* suggests), Forster was pessimistic about man in an organised community even if not about man in his individual state. But muddle, not original sin, was the enemy, and he never tempered his humanism to the winds of the revived Christian salvationism that blew for a brief while in the post-war years. His distrust of community, although at present it makes him seem retrogressive, is understandable. We have learned a little how to live together in small groups; we have yet to learn how to organise ourselves humanely in the greater ones.

Sadness, rather than pessimism, is the prevailing tone in much of Forster's writing, an elegiac note in part accountable by the length of his life. But, even so, the melancholy set in early. His uprooting from Rooksnest affected him deeply; and the nostalgia for the lost, because never-to-be-found, beloved, which haunts so much covert homosexual writing during his early years (Housman being its supreme exponent), in Forster's case invested its emotion in grief for a rural England threatened and departing. But it is an essentially personal grief: hence, perhaps the uncharacteristically lush lyricism of the descriptive passages in *Howards End*. Certainly it is what makes him in part a Georgian: this kind of sensitivity to rural life, a whimsical or enervating perspective on the past, pervades the first two decades of the century. It took T. S. Eliot and Ezra Pound to vitalise and renew this retrospective vision, and to widen its horizons beyond that of rural England – and to their names should be added those of John Cowper Powys and David Jones, for both of whom 'mythology' and 'tradition' were more than merely literary matters.[5] Powys indeed shares with Forster rather more than might be imagined, considering the difference in their literary methods and concerns – notably a refusal to settle for either an optimistic or a pessimistic point of view, dislike of authoritarianism and distrust of scientific method when applied to human beings, sympathy with the outsider and the loner and with ordinary people, belief in the sacredness of domestic life, a carelessness about literary prestige, and a compassionate tolerance that seems likely to outlast convictions based more narrowly. In both writers a sense of the past is a necessary accompaniment to a full response to life.

Forster's work in this kind lacks the sense of history that we find in Eliot, Pound and Jones: in this respect his insistence on the supreme value of the individual is limiting. But that very concern, together with its extension into more general terms, accounts for his continuing influence. The way in which, in the novels, he works through his own predicament illuminates his final position as a humanist spokesman. The life-in-death he allots to Philip Herriton becomes that of the narrator in *A Passage to India*; in the words of I. A. Richards, 'he has stepped back to the position of the observer from which . . . he was at such pains to eject his Philip'.[6] In between he had posited affirmation through self-sacrifice (*The Longest Journey*), affirmation through the leap of faith (*A Room with a View* and *Maurice*), and in *Howards End* had blundered (it is hard not to use the word) through a web of complication to a resolution that was not quite the one he presumably intended.[7] But, if *A Passage to India* constitutes a partial defeat for moral idealism, it is a triumph for artistic integrity. The book itself, not its message, gives one hope. Much time has been devoted to what Forster thought and had to say, and yet, 'How do I know what I think till I see what I say?' The principle holds good for art. Forster's later examinations of the function and limits of social order, which show his sympathy with what the Wilcox world stands for at its best, were the outcome of an initial artistic struggle. Here, in aesthetic achievement, not in moral pronouncements, are his credentials as a voice to be attended to.

That voice speaks to our uncertainties: as Malcolm Bradbury suggests, 'It is because . . . he is not a novelist of solutions, because his fiction proposes incompleteness, that he seems to us modern.'[8] His influence, by-passing the modernist mainstream of James Joyce and Virginia Woolf (is it, in fact, a mainstream at all?), can be seen in novelists as different as Christopher Isherwood, L. P. Hartley, Henry Green and Angus Wilson, all of whom have explored the realm of psychic and emotional injury and the principles of renewal as they are found in failure and defeat. His technical experimentation is most clearly reflected in the work of Green, but his influence on all four writers shows how diverse and fructifying his achievement was to be.

He has been called a visionary novelist; and, although there are good grounds for this, the attribution still seems faintly wrong. For Forster lacked the single-mindedness, the narrowness even, of the true visionary: looking at the flowers distracted him – unless you consider that to be the visionary's true business – and he did not seek in any way to unite his soul with them. However, it is worth pointing out that the criticism implied in the following comment on Virginia Woolf is made from the point of view of one who sees that union as at least a possibility: 'she is always stretching out from her enchanted tree and snatching bits from the flux of daily life as they float past, and out of those bits she builds novels. She would not plunge. And she should not have plunged.'[9]

The essentially lightweight character of Forster's own other-worldly intimations prevented him likewise from taking that plunge; he was not one to sound such supernatural dimensions as may exist, and his poetic prose has a self-consciousness, a looking-two-ways quality which is unconvincing. And yet these very uncertainties, these ambiguities of venture and withdrawal, speak to our condition in a way that the robust affirmations of Browning, say, or Meredith can no longer do. Forster's refusal to lay hold on dogmatism for support can yet prove a timely example in a period when the upholders of tradition may be tempted, in its defence, to do just that. 'I do not believe in Belief.' The statement is either strong or sloppy. Much may depend on how we decide we shall interpret it.

Forster's literary status is, in purely literary terms, secure. Although not a novelist on the scale, either in performance or intent, of Conrad, Lawrence, Joyce or Powys, he is more generally popular than any of them. But 'great'? Is Jane Austen 'great'? That word's usefulness is limited where art is concerned, for it is bound up with a sense of scale. It is a spatial category: so too with 'major', 'perfect' and 'profound'. Rather it is the quality of livingness that we should look for, a feeling of supra-temporal value induced by the vitalising relationship of the work's various elements. The musicality of Forster's novels is an example of this, organising as it does the imaginative obsessions from which they were conceived. The occasion of those obsessions, the need to resolve the tension between guilt and rebellion where his sexual nature was concerned, enacts the myth of human growth, moving from undifferentiated being into a harmonious relationship with the mother (a process recorded in the novels up to *Howards End*), and so through to the assertion of the independent will in separation (*Maurice* and the later tales): the final maturity of reintegration with the origins of his imagination at the conscious level is in Forster's case achieved in *A Passage to India*. And this personal progress is representative of social conditions as well: the waverings, within the progress, between rebellion and acceptance are a continuing movement observable as societies renew themselves. No one truth provides a resting place, unless it be the consciousness of life and death in each individual by which the validity of every institution must be judged. Forster, like all major writers, is constantly aware of this point of reference and he raised it in an early, unpublished tale, 'The Rock'.[10]

In this story a man who has been rescued from drowning by a boatload of Cornish fishermen, at no cost to themselves, is faced with the question, 'What price do you set on your own life?' To reward them adequately seems impossible. The story presents the total dissocation of the world of money values and the world of human values. The man's solution of his problem is to offer his rescuers precisely nothing, and, having sold all his goods and given the money away, to throw himself on their charity in a gesture of despair. Time finally does its work, and after much suffering he is accepted by them. The little fable voices the predicament that Forster, with so many others, has seen as lying behind our materialistic, irreligious society (the words are not used here pejoratively): any utilitarian approach to moral values is in the end nonsensical. So too is the attempt to rationalise concern for individual life. For, if that concern is denied, Forster would say, then all else worthwhile is denied with it, since we have lost our only possible referend of meaning.

For all its limitations, it is the mythopoeic nature of Forster's imagination which gives him his timeless quality. A minor novelist dates; a major one forces us to ask ourselves if *we* have dated. The question raised by John Beer, in what remains one of the most sensitive accounts of Forster's work, is therefore vital. Summing up Forster's position in the light of post-war social change, he remarks that the two wars have 'destroyed that stable social scene which is the bulwark of his comedy, while subsequent disillusionment and cynicism have sapped assurance from the romanticism which has been a mainstay of his vision. Only his moral position is left untouched.'[11]

Beer's comment was applied to Forster's failure to write any more fiction in his later years; but it is relevant to the question why we read him now. Although we may find that the romance has dated, the comedy endures: social change is transcended by art. And the clash between the two elements, which disconcerted his contemporaries, has resolved itself at the expense of the romance. The artistic expression of the novels and stories is thus often flawed for us by the conflict between a convincing prose and a passion which we cannot quite endorse. But the moral vision, the good humour, intelligence and sanity are unaffected. Forster himself had a strong feeling that civilisation as he knew it was probably doomed; but he knew how to distinguish between that civilisation and its outward effects. In the Rede Lecture on Virginia Woolf he observed that she belonged to 'an age which distinguished sharply between the impermanency of man and the durability of his monuments'.[12] He himself was under no illusions as to the durability of monuments; but he continued to believe in the permanent moral potential of man, though well aware of what man was capable of becoming, or of doing to the world. This did not cause him to despair, or to lower his standards; he believed in truth, not on his terms but on its own. This fidelity to the civilised ideal which he had found as a young man when he came up to Cambridge is what makes him great, and what secures for him the admiration as well as the affection of posterity.

He is with all the men and women who have sought something in life that is neither chaos nor mechanism, who have not confused happiness with possessiveness, or victory with success, and who have believed in love.[13]

The words that he wrote to honour Mahatma Gandhi define his own achievement too.

Notes

INTRODUCTION

1 *The Diary of Virginia Woolf*, vol. I, ed. Anne Olivier Bell (1977), p. 291.
2 Ibid., p. 295.
3 F. R. Leavis, *The Common Pursuit* (1952), pp. 261–7.
4 Quoted in P. N. Furbank, *E. M. Forster: A Life*, vol. II (1978), p. 2.
5 Quoted Ibid., p. 163.

CHAPTER ONE

1 'A brief analysis of Chattering Hassocks has survived: fifty lions and as many unicorns sit upon hassocks, and the lions put forward a plea for tolerance and for variety of opinion which I still support' (*Marianne Thornton*, p. 271, note).
2 'The Challenge of Our Time', *Two Cheers for Democracy*.
3 *The Longest Journey*, The World's Classics edition (1960), p. xii.
4 Forster's history of Sawston does not altogether tally with that of Tonbridge: he has loaded the dice against his old school. For the actual facts, see D. C. Somervell, *A History of Tonbridge School* (1947).
5 A comparison of *Where Angels Fear to Tread* (the proofs of which he read at Nassenheide) with 'Elizabeth's' own later novel *The Enchanted April* (1922) is instructive. In both books the Italian landscape exposes the frigid repressions of the English temperament; but, whereas for Forster this comes as a process of moral judgement and sharp humour, 'Elizabeth' dissolves everything in charm. Her book is gay, and frequently witty; but it interprets Italy simply as an alternative to English life, not as a power with which to reckon. Her last novel, *Mr Skeffington*, a best-seller like her first, was published in 1941, seventeen years after *A Passage to India*; but to the end of her writing life 'Elizabeth' remained an Edwardian. Forster was never merely that.
6 *Pall Mall Gazette*, 28 Oct 1910. Quoted in Philip Gardner, *E. M. Forster: The Critical Heritage* (1973), pp. 126–7.
7 Quoted in P. N. Furbank, *E. M. Forster: A Life*, vol. I (1977), p. 218.
8 Ibid., p. 190.
9 Quoted in Oliver Stallybrass, Introduction to *Aspects of the Novel*, Abinger Edition (1974), p. xi.
10 Laurence Brander, *E. M. Forster: A Critical Study* (1968), p. 4.
11 Christopher Isherwood, *Down There on a Visit* (1962), p. 77.
12 Christopher Isherwood, *Christopher and His Kind* (1977), p. 84.
13 See Alec Randall, 'Forster in Rumania', in *Aspects of E. M. Forster*, ed. Oliver Stallybrass (1969).

175

14 Richard Martin, *The Love That Failed: Ideal and Reality in the Writings of E. M. Forster* (The Hague, 1974), p. 186, note 10.
15 'The Last of Abinger', *Two Cheers for Democracy*. Characteristically this is made up of jottings from his commonplace book over a period of just under twenty years.
16 William Plomer, 'Forster as a Friend', in *Aspects of Forster,* ed. (Stallybrass, p. 102).

CHAPTER TWO

1 Philip Larkin, 'The Building', *High Windows* (1974), p. 24.
2 See G. K. Chesterton, *The Victorian Age in Literature* (1913).
3 In addition to opening the way for universal education, the government had introduced entry to the Civil Service by examination, abolished the purchase and sale of commissions in the armed services, admitted Dissenters to the universities and instituted the secret ballot.
4 'The Challenge of Our Time', *Two Cheers for Democracy*.
5 Plomer, 'Forster as a Friend', in *Aspects of Forster*, ed. Stallybrass, p. 102.
6 *Aspects of the Novel*, Ch. 5: 'The Plot'.

CHAPTER THREE

1 Brander, *Forster: A Critical Study*, p. 14.
2 Foreword to *Goldsworthy Lowes Dickinson*, Abinger Edition (1973).
3 In *Forster: The Critical Heritage*, ed. Philip Gardner, p. 419.
4 *Aspects of the Novel*, Abinger Edition, Appendix B, p. 139.
5 Ibid., p. 129.
6 Ibid., p. 126.
7 These essays were reprinted in *Abinger Harvest*.
8 Reprinted in *Two Cheers for Democracy*.
9 'Morality and the Novel', *Selected Literary Criticism,* ed. Anthony Beal (1955).

CHAPTER FOUR

1 The artist was Charles Sims (1873–1928), a popular painter of landscapes, portraits and allegorical subjects.
2 *Selected Literary Criticism*, ed. Beal, p. 118.
3 Wilfred Stone, *The Cave and the Mountain* (Oxford, 1965) p. 123.
4 Ibid., p. 124.
5 Max Beerbohm, *Seven Men* (1919).
6 Mildred Peaslake: the name is worthy of Firbank. Peaslake is a village not far from Abinger.
7 John Colmer, *E. M. Forster: The Personal Voice* (1975) p. 26.
8 Stone, *The Cave and the Mountain*, p. 157.
9 It was not reprinted until 1972, in *The Life to Come.*
10 Howard was also the name of a family who formerly lived at Rooksnest. Forster was to put it to more complimentary use in his fourth novel.
11 Lionel Trilling, *E. M. Forster: A Study* (1944), p. 42.

12 Reprinted in *A Variety of Things* (1928).
13 George H. Thomson, *The Fiction of E. M. Forster* (Detroit, 1967), p. 59.
14 J. B. Beer, *The Achievement of E. M. Forster* (1962), p. 45.
15 Raymond Williams, *The English Novel from Dickens to Lawrence* (1970),
     p. 138.

CHAPTER FIVE

1 Colmer, *Forster: The Personal Voice*, p. 16.
2 Norman Douglas, *South Wind* (1917), Ch. 3.
3 Elizabeth Bowen, 'A Passage to Forster', in *Aspects of Forster,* ed. Stally-
    brass, p. 6.

CHAPTER SIX

1 *The Longest Journey*, The World's Classics edition, p. ix.
2 Ibid., p. ii.
3 Ibid., p. ix.
4 Alan Wilde, *Art And Order: A Study of E. M. Forster* (New York, 1964)
    p. 35, note.
5 In *Forster: The Critical Heritage*, ed. Gardner, pp. 77–8.
6 Frederick C. Crews, *E. M. Forster: The Perils of Humanism* (Oxford,
    1962), p. 58.
7 Trilling, *Forster: A Study*, p. 67.

CHAPTER SEVEN

1 The two 'Lucy' fragments were published in 1977 in the Abinger Edition,
    vol. IIIa, in a limited edition of 1000 copies, as *The Lucy Novels*, ed. Oliver
    Stallybrass.
2 'The way that women behaved, when they thought no-one was observing
    them, sent him off into fits of uncontrollable laughter. It amused him
    enormously to watch them running for a bus, diving earnestly into their
    handbags, making up their faces with the aid of a pocket mirror, adjusting
    their hats' – Sewell Stokes, 'Reminiscences of Ronald Firbank', in *Ronald
    Firbank: Memoirs and Critiques*, ed. Mervyn Horder (1977), pp. 130–1.
3 Crews, *Forster: The Perils of Humanism*, p. 81.
4 Rose Macaulay, *The Writings of E. M. Forster* (1938), pp. 88–9.
5 See Furbank, *Forster: A Life*, vol. II, pp. 3–4.
6 Jeffrey Meyers, *Homosexuality and Literature 1890–1930* (1977), pp.
    92–5.

CHAPTER EIGHT

1 For a detailed exposition of the country-house theme in twentieth-century
    English literature, see Richard Gill, *Happy Rural Seat: The English
    Country House and the Literary Imagination* (1972).
2 Trilling, *Forster: A Study*, p. 102.

3 16 June 1908. Quoted by Stallybrass in Introduction to *Howards End*, Abinger Edition (1973).
4 Letter to Forster, 20 Sep 1922.
5 Poynton is yet another mansion to go up in smoke, spoils and all.
6 23 Dec 1898. Quoted in Leon Edel, *Henry James: The Treacherous Years 1895–1900* (1969), p. 245.
7 David Cecil, *Poets and Story-tellers* (1949), p. 184.
8 Mention should be made here of Forster's pageant play, *England's Pleasant Land* (1940). Here we find no romantic nostalgia, only a biting indignation against the Enclosers and later the Developers, the latter destroying the beauty which, ironically, the former had created. But the play no more confronts the paradox than does *Howards End*. Lamentation and anger never quite fuse in Forster's work.
9 Introduction to *Howards End*, Abinger Edition, p. xiv.
10 K. W. Gransden, *E. M. Forster* (1962), p. 68.
11 Macaulay, *Writings of Forster*, p. 107.
12 Brander, *Forster: A Critical Study*, p. 162.
13 'The Challenge of Our Time', *Two Cheers for Democracy*.

CHAPTER NINE

1 12 Feb 1915.
2 S. Hynes, *Edwardian Occasions: Essays on English Writing in the Early Twentieth Century* (1972), p. 115.
3 H. J. Oliver, *The Art of E. M. Forster* (Melbourne, 1960), p. 31.
4 Hynes, *Edwardian Occasions*, p. 119.
5 *A Passage to India*, Ch. 14.
6 G. Steiner, 'Under the Greenwood Tree', in *Forster: The Critical Heritage*, ed. Gardner, p. 481.
7 Colmer, *Forster: The Personal Voice*, p. 114.
8 John Saye Martin, *E. M. Forster: The Endless Journey* (1976), p. 164.
9 In *Forster: The Critical Heritage*, ed. Gardner, p. 480.
10 I. A. Richards, 'A Passage To Forster: Reflections on a Novelist', in *Forster: A Collection of Critical Essays*, ed. Malcolm Bradbury (1966), p. 18.
11 Forrest Reid, *Apostate* (1926), Ch. 10.
12 Quoted in Stallybrass, Introduction to *The Life to Come*, p. xii.
13 Meyers, *Homosexuality and Literature*, p. 108.

CHAPTER TEN

1 *The Nation and Athenaeum*, 21 Jan 1922. Quoted in G. K. Das, *E. M. Forster's India* (1977), p. 21.
2 N. C. Chaudhuri, 'A Passage to and from India', *Encounter*, 11 June 1964.
3 Macaulay, *Writings of Forster*, pp. 188–90.
4 Note to *A Passage to India*, Everyman's Library edition (1942). Mr P. N. Furbank tells me that Peter Burra's Introduction to this edition was the one critical account of which Forster wholeheartedly approved.
5 Das, *Forster's India*, p. 43.

6 'Pondicherry', *The Hill of Devi*.
7 'Gokul Ashtami', ibid.
8 In *Forster: The Critical Heritage*, ed. Gardner, pp. 480–1.
9 For a full account of the book's reception, see Das, *Forster's India*.
10 'The Mission of Hinduism', *Daily News and Leader*, 30 Apr 1915, quoted ibid., p. 5.
11 'Adrift in India': '1. The Nine Gems of Ujjain', *Abinger Harvest*.
12 Wilde, *Art and Order*, p. 151.
13 Introduction to *To the Lighthouse*, Everyman's Library edition (1938), p. xii.

CONCLUSION

1 Patrick Wilkinson, 'Forster and King's', in *Aspects of Forster*, ed., Stallybrass, pp. 26–7.
2 Trilling, *Forster: A Study*, p. 10.
3 Reprinted in *Two Cheers for Democracy*.
4 12 Feb 1915.
5 Jones, indeed, precisely because he is of part-Welsh descent and not American, is of greater relevance to the purely English tradition than are his two better-known fellow poets.
6 In *Forster: A Collection of Critical Essays*, ed. Bradbury, p. 17.
7 '. . . the whole direction of the novel as a narrative pattern (running counter, as so often in Forster, to the dabbed-on generalisations) shows that money or property may be a more important inheritance than ideas' – Gransden, *Forster*, p. 57.
8 Op. cit., p. 4.
9 *Two Cheers for Democracy*.
10 The tale is discussed by Forster in the Introduction to *The Collected Short Stories* (1947) but was not reprinted until *The Life to Come* (1972).
11 In *Forster: A Collection of Critical Essays*, ed. Bradbury, p. 205.
12 *Two Cheers for Democracy*.
13 *Mahatma Gandhi: Essays and Reflections on His Life and Work, Together with a New Memorial Section*, ed. S. Radhakrishnan (1949), pp. 386–8. Printed as Appendix A in Das, *Forster's India*.

Bibliography

1. Principal works by E. M. Forster

1905 *Where Angels Fear to Tread* (novel)
1907 *The Longest Journey* (novel)
1908 *A Room with a View* (novel)
1910 *Howards End* (novel)
1911 *The Celestial Omnibus* (short stories)
    Contains 'The Story of a Panic', 'The Other Side of the Hedge', 'The Celestial Omnibus', 'Other Kingdom', 'The Curate's Friend', 'The Road from Colonus'.
1922 *Alexandria: A History and a Guide* (guidebook)
1923 *Pharos and Pharillon* (essays)
1924 *A Passage to India* (novel)
1927 *Aspects of the Novel* (criticism)
1928 *The Eternal Moment* (short stories)
    Contains 'The Machine Stops', 'The Point of It', 'Mr Andrews', 'Co-ordination', 'The Story of the Siren', The Eternal Moment'.
1934 *Goldsworthy Lowes Dickinson* (biography)
1936 *Abinger Harvest* (essays)
1940 *England's Pleasant Land* (pageant play)
1951 *Two Cheers for Democracy* (essays)
1953 *The Hill of Devi* (biography)
1956 *Marianne Thornton* (biography)
1971 *Maurice* (novel)
1972 *The Life to Come* (short stories)
    Contains 'Ansell', 'Albergo Empedocle', 'The Purple Envelope', 'The Helping Hand', 'The Rock', 'The Life to Come', 'Dr Woolacott', 'Arthur Snatchfold', 'The Obelisk', 'What Does It Matter? A Morality', 'The Classical Annex', 'The Torque', 'The Other Boat', 'Three Courses and a Dessert' ('The Second Course' by Forster)

2. A Selection of Critical and Biographical Sources

(* denotes book-length studies of Forster. Except where otherwise stated, the place of publication is London)

1934 Frank Swinnerton, *The Georgian Literary Scene*
1938 Cyril Connolly, *Enemies of Promise*
    Dorothy M. Hoare, *Some Studies in the Modern Novel*
    Rose Macaulay, *The Writings of E. M. Forster**
1941 Virginia Woolf, *The Death of the Moth*

1944 Lionel Trilling, *E. M. Forster: A Study**

1947 Christopher Isherwood, *Lions and Shadows*

1949 David Cecil, *Poets and Story-tellers*

1950 Elizabeth Bowen, *Collected Impressions*
      Rex Warner, *E. M. Forster*

1952 F. R. Leavis, *The Common Pursuit*

1953 G. S. Fraser, *The Modern Writer and his World*
      Stephen Spender, *The Creative Element.*

1954 J. K. Johnstone, *The Bloomsbury Group*

1955 Walter Allen, *The English Novel*

1957 D. J. Enright, *The Apothecary's Shop: Essays on Literature*
      James McConkey, *The Novels of E. M. Forster* (Ithaca, NY)*

1958 P. N. Furbank and F. J. H. Haskell, *Writers at Work. The Paris Review
      Interviews*

1960 H. J. Oliver, *The Art of E. M. Forster* (Melbourne)*
      Leonard Woolf, *Sowing: An Autobiography of the Years 1880–1904*

1962 J. B. Beer, *The Achievement of E. M. Forster*
      Frederick C. Crews, *E. M. Forster: The Perils of Humanism* (Princeton,
      NJ)*
      K. W. Gransden, *E. M. Forster**
      Leonard Woolf, *Growing: An Autobiography of the Years 1904–1911*

1963 C. B. Cox, *The Free Spirit: A Study of Liberalism and Humanism in the
      Novels of George Eliot, Henry James, E. M. Forster, Virginia Woolf,
      Angus Wilson*

1964 Barbara Hardy, *The Appropriate Form: An Essay on the Novel*
      K. Natwar-Singh (ed.), *E. M. Forster: A Tribute. With Selections from
      his Writings on India* (New York)*
      Alan Wilde, *Art and Order: A Study of E. M. Forster* (New York)*
      Leonard Woolf, *Beginning Again: An Autobiography of the Years
      1911–1918*

1965 B. J. A. Kirkpatrick, *A Bibliography of E. M. Forster*
      Harry T. Moore, *E. M. Forster* (New York)*
      V. S. Pritchett, *The Living Novel*
      David Shusterman, *The Quest for Certitude in E. M. Forster's Fiction*
      (Bloomington, Ind.)*

1966 Malcolm Bradbury (ed.), *Forster: A Collection of Critical Essays*
      Wilfred Stone, *The Cave and the Mountain: A Study of E. M. Forster*
      (Stanford, Calif.)*

1967 Norman Kelvin, *E. M. Forster* (Carbondale, Ill.)*
      George H. Thomson, *The Fiction of E. M. Forster* (Detroit)*
      Leonard Woolf, *Downhill All the Way: An Autobiography of the Years
      1919–1939*

1968 Quentin Bell, *Bloomsbury*
      Laurence Brander, *E. M. Forster; A Critical Study**
      Denis Godfrey, *E. M. Forster's Other Kingdom**
      Samuel Hynes, *The Edwardian Frame of Mind*

1969 H. H. Gowda (ed.), *A Garland for E. M. Forster* (Mysore)
      Stuart Hampshire, *Modern Writers and Other Essays*
      Frederick P. W. McDowell, *E. M. Forster* (New York)*
      Oliver Stallybrass (ed.), *Aspects of E. M. Forster*

1970 J. R. Ackerley, *E. M. Forster. A Portrait*
1972 Samuel Hynes, *Edwardian Occasions: Essays on English Writing in the Early Twentieth Century*
     Richard Gill, *Happy Rural Seat: The English Country House and the Literary Imagination*
1973 Philip Gardner (ed.), *E. M. Forster: The Critical Heritage*
1974 Richard Martin, *The Love That Failed: Idea and Reality in the Writings of E. M. Forster* (The Hague)*
1975 John Colmer, *E. M. Forster: The Personal Voice**
1977 John Saye Martin, *E. M. Forster: The Endless Journey**
     Christopher Isherwood, *Christopher and His Kind*
     Jeffrey Meyers, *Homosexuality and Literature 1890–1930*
     G. K. Das, *E. M. Forster's India*
     P. N. Furbank, *E. M. Forster: A Life,* vol. I: *The Growth of the Novelist 1879–1914.*
1978 P. N. Furbank, *E. M. Forster: A Life,* vol. II: *Polycrates' Ring 1914–1970.*
     Francis King, *E. M. Forster and His World**

Index

184   *A Reading of E. M. Forster*